The Healthy Marketing Handbook

Mike Clarke

Published in 2022 by FeedARead.com Publishing

A CIP catalogue record for this title is available from the British Library.

Dedicated to my amazing wife Naomi, and our two wonderful kids, Nia and John.

I’m blessed to have you as my family.

x

Buyer-only Bonus

To access a free audio version of this book, narrated by the author, visit:

www.healthymarketer.me/book

Contents

Introduction

"There are three things that could be causing your son's illness," the consultant explained to my wife and I as we both sat nervously on the edge of the hospital bed, our hands resting lightly on our son's legs that were hidden underneath the blanket.

"It could be a virus..."

That's manageable, I thought to myself instantly.

"It could be juvenile arthritis..."

Sounds nasty, but okay, we'll take that, I quickly determined in my head.

"Or it could be leukaemia."

Bam.

A metaphorical anvil had just been swung quietly in from the side of the cubicle, smashing into my head and leaving me reeling.

Time stopped.

A jolt of horror raced through my entire body, from head to toes. Then it raced back again, from toes to head.

Ding! Ding!

Total knockout.

Leukaemia.

There it was. The unspeakable worry had just been spoken.

A parent's worst nightmare had become reality in those five words.

"Or it could be leukaemia."

Leukaemia.

Cancer.

Our son.

Our son.

Our *son.*

And just like that, one day later, a diagnosis of acute lymphoblastic leukaemia (ALL) was confirmed.

As you might imagine, life changed for us as a family suddenly and dramatically with that diagnosis. Our son was six and a half years old at the time, our daughter eight.

The treatment required for boys with ALL was three and a half years (!!) of chemotherapy. The first phase would be aggressive treatment to completely eradicate the cancer from the body.

The following phase, known as ‘maintenance’, would be gentler (in theory, anyway) and focused on ensuring the cancer did not come back.

For the next three and a half years, normal life was put on pause.

Colours seemed dimmer, while everyday sounds seemed somehow muffled and more distant.

The noise and laughter that had previously filled our home was replaced by long, unsettling periods of stillness and quiet, followed by sounds of retching and us rushing to our son’s side to clear up the mess and to hug him.

Our sobs for our son were often unheard, somehow held inside us while we hugged him and told him we were there for him.

Normal life was quickly nothing more than just a memory.

Seeing other people out and about, enjoying holidays, exercise, family days out, was a weird experience, like looking at an alternative world or a faint memory of a long-forgotten past.

During that time, we all became far more familiar than we ever wanted to be with different chemotherapy medicines and treatments.

With hospitals and Oncology wards.

Emergency admissions, blood tests and transfusions.

Jumping out of bed at all times of the night whenever we heard our son calling for help.

We all became experts in platelets, neutrophils, white and red blood cells, knowing which numbers were 'good' and which were 'bad'.

My wife and I both spent countless nights trying to sleep on the fold-up spare bed in the hospital room. (We were always in an individual hospital room because the chemotherapy lowered our son’s immune system and made him much more vulnerable to any bugs and infections.)

Fortunately, our son's treatment was successful. At the time of writing this book, he has been cancer-free for three years.

In many ways, it seems like another life. In others, it seems like only yesterday.

Looking back on that painful, confusing, traumatic, and exhausting time, we are so very grateful to all the people who were involved in his care, and those who supported us as individuals and as a family; emotionally, mentally, physically, and spiritually.

Family, friends, friends of friends, friends of friends’ friends, NHS staff, our lovely church family in Bristol (highgrove.church if you want to check them out).

And even though time helps to make even the most painful memories fade somewhat, our family still has the mental scars.

They will always be with us. And they will always influence and affect how we see everyday life.

What kind of business book is this, anyway?

At this point, you may well be wondering why on earth I started a business marketing book with such a personal (and still painful to describe) story about our son's childhood cancer diagnosis and treatment.

As a marketer, shouldn't I have begun by proclaiming my inarguable marketing genius? By telling a "rags to riches" story that cleverly highlighted my undoubted brilliance in an unassuming, incredibly humble "gee, shucks" way?

Or couldn't I have started by jumping in with all my metaphorical marketing guns blazing, written bullets quickly chewing up and eliminating the unhealthy mess that is much of modern marketing?

Why didn't I fire a bunker-busting downloadable PDF called "**The 10 Things You MUST Know Before Hiring A Marketer**" towards you, to polish my credentials as somebody who knows *exactly* how the marketing guru game is played?

I'm sure I *could* have done any of those, but unlike the authors of many marketing and copywriting books nowadays, I like to base myself firmly in reality.

Please take it from me, I am most certainly *not* some marketing genius who has nobly descended from on high, given as a gift to the world to demonstrate my business profit-making superiority over mere marketing mortals.

(REALITY CHECK: If I even tried to do that, my wife and kids would happily – and quite rightly - bring me back down to earth with a profound and well-deserved bump.)

I do however have *some* knowledge that you might not have.

Some experiences you *won't* have had.

And I believe I may be able to help improve the health of your marketing.

I'm gonna make you a deal you can't refuse…

So, here's the deal. As you read this book, please read it in the manner it has been written.

Think of it as a conversation with a friend, maybe over a drink (say, a nicely chilled glass of white wine?), about a *different way of thinking*.

As you read, please know that there is no pressure, no "hard selling" and definitely no attempt to convince you why I am "RIGHT", and you are "WRONG".

Please do *not* think of it as a lecture or proclamation by some self-appointed marketing guru, who alone has all the solutions to any and all marketing problems. (How arrogant would I have to be to believe that?)

That's not my way. That has never been my way. It will *never* be my way.

(If you're looking for that kind of thing, a simple online search for terms like '*marketing expert*', '*marketing guru*', or '*best copywriter*' will give you plenty of results to start working your way through. That approach does come with a significant health warning though. Unfortunately, there will always be plenty of unscrupulous people more than happy to extract money from your wallet without giving you anything of value in return.)

Having said that, I am trying to sell something to you through this book.

A monthly £5,000 coaching programme!

(Just kidding.)

No, I'm trying to sell you on a *healthier way of thinking about marketing*.

If I succeed in my aim, I'll be delighted.

If I fail, I hope that at least I'll have made you stop and think about things.

And hey, even if you disagree with everything you read in this book, I completely respect that. I'll still talk to you! After all, if we both agreed on everything, one of us would be unnecessary.

If you'd like to improve the health of your marketing, to strengthen your business, to build it up and make it more resilient and future-proofed…then this book may be just what you've been looking for.

Why should you listen to me?

But why on earth should anyone listen to me (especially when I struggle to get our two teenagers to listen to me sometimes)?

Despite definitely not being a marketing guru, I have a "slightly-different-to-the-normal" background which gives me a unique marketing perspective. One that may benefit you and your business.

As a teenager, I loved all things to do with health and fitness. Protein shakes, following the workouts in a book for people training to become Royal Marine Commandos, countless pull-ups, sit-ups, squats, walks with weighted rucksack, even jogs with weighted ankle wraps.

I did them all.

A lot.

For several years, I seriously considered joining the armed forces. Fortunately for the defence of our nation, I didn't.

After A-levels, I studied at the University of Wales College of Medicine and obtained a BSc (Hons) in Diagnostic Radiography.

I then worked for several years in the National Health Service (NHS) in the United Kingdom as a Diagnostic Radiographer. (That's the person in a hospital who takes X-rays, CT, MRI, and ultrasound scans. They produce the diagnostic images that consultant radiologists then use to assess a problem, to diagnose a disease or illness, to determine the extent of any damage to the body, or to see how the body is responding to treatment.)

Following years of night shifts, on-calls and hundreds of hours working in A&E and operating theatres, I transitioned into working as a medical sales representative where I spent my days talking with consultants and general practitioners about different medical treatments.

During that time, I gained a heck of a lot of experience in face-to-face selling.

Of gaining access to people through gatekeepers (are there any more effective gatekeepers than medical secretaries?).

Of persuading and influencing using accurate, provable data (no flim-flam selling for me!).

I then decided to do something that was an obvious career move to absolutely nobody and became a professional magician for nearly a decade. That's right - from medical sales representative to professional magician. Take it from me, that is quite a big change.

What can I say? I like to keep my parents on their toes. (Mum and Dad, I love you guys!)

Working for nine and a half years as a professional magician gave me an incredibly deep, comprehensive, real-world education in persuasion and influence, in marketing and copywriting.

In how to sell using nothing but words.

I lived or died, metaphorically, from the results I generated. If what I did worked, I would make money and be kept busy. If I failed, I would not make much money and would be spending a lot of time at home!

I discovered from experience how to adapt and adjust my manner, the words I used, the pace I spoke at, the energy I drew on and used, the way I held my body, even the way I dressed, in order to create the best results from my shows.

I tested, measured and adjusted different approaches to marketing myself, seeing what worked and what didn't.

During those nine and a half years, I spent thousands of hours entertaining many tens of thousands of people.

I mastered the art of misdirection during my performances, directing people to look in one direction while the real work went on elsewhere.

I also invested thousands of hours (*and many thousands of pounds!*) educating myself about marketing, persuasion, the psychology of change, copywriting, influence and selling.

I flew to the US twice for specialist training, once with the world leader in infotainment and selling from the platform.

For more than 20 years, I have been a *serious* student of marketing and direct-response copywriting (that's a fancy way of describing commercial writing that actually delivers measurable results).

An invitation

Everything described and discussed in this book has been used by me personally to generate money for my businesses and the people who have hired me.

Having seen the difference these principles have made, I will *always* be somebody who approaches marketing in a healthy way.

I will always be a healthy marketer.

This book is an invitation for you to become a healthy marketer too.

But what the heck *is* healthy marketing anyway? You'll find out in chapter two.

Before we get there though, we've got a stop to make on the way.

A rather unexpected stop.

Chapter One –
An Unexpected Trip

To help set the scene for the rest of this book, we're going to do something a bit unexpected. (I'm a big fan of what NLP refers to as 'pattern interrupts' – doing something unusual to shock people into behavioural change.)

For that reason, would you mind falling down your stairs* please?

** In your imagination only! Please do NOT actually throw yourself down the stairs – that would be foolish. I'm pretty good at painting a picture with words, but I'm not liable if you willingly choose to throw yourself down your stairs…*

That's right.

I'd like you to <u>imagine</u> that you are walking down your stairs first thing one morning when you have a fall.

Maybe your foot caught on one of the steps? Perhaps the thought of your morning coffee momentarily distracted you as you were placing your foot down?

Or maybe, and more likely, you're not quite sure what happened?

All you *do* know for certain is that you are now lying in a crumpled heap at the bottom of your stairs, somewhat shocked to find yourself in such an unusual and uncomfortable position.

As you begin to recover from the initial shock, you try to do a quick mental assessment of your body to determine whether it's safe for you to try to move.

You know that you didn't bang your head, and your hips are both feeling okay, so after a few more seconds of contemplation, you begin wriggling yourself into a more composed position.

This is not easy to do in such a limited space, so it takes a few heaves and grunts (and muttered words under your breath) before you are able to get yourself moving.

You shuffle yourself into a sitting position, then begin trying to stand. If somebody was watching you do this, it would look more comical than elegant.

As you raise yourself, you quickly realise that your left ankle is feeling a bit odd.

In fact, as you think about it more, you notice that it is really *very* painful indeed. Particularly as you place more weight onto it as you continue to stand.

Despite this unexpected pain, you somehow manage to pull yourself into a half-standing, half-hopping position, and cling firmly to the bannister for support.

After a few half-hearted attempts to put your left leg down more firmly on the floor, you determine that you won't be able to put any weight on your left leg for a while, because it causes too much pain in your ankle.

In fact, as you look at your ankle, you're pretty sure it's looking bigger than usual. Almost like somebody has inflated it just like they would have a balloon.

Hmmm…

At this point, you realise that whatever plans you had for the day have been scuppered. No morning coffee for a start (darn it!).

Even though you try to second guess yourself and attempt to come up with excuses not to do this, you realise that you're going to need to go to the local hospital to see if you've - big breath - *broken* anything.

Whether you're able to get your partner, your husband or wife, a neighbour or a friend to give you a lift, or you need to arrange a taxi to take you there, you know that your next stop is going to be the hospital.

This was *not* on your daily schedule. And it is most definitely an unwelcome change to your day.

Somehow you manage to hobble from the stairs to your front door, then down your front path and onto the pavement, whereupon you fall into the car with all the grace of a toddler trying to walk on ice.

Although your entry into the car was far from graceful, you're just happy to be sitting down and able to rest your ankle.

During the drive, it's all you can do to stop crying out in pain because your ankle is just *so* painful. Every bump in the road causes a sharp stab of pain to shoot around your ankle.

During the journey, you try to remember and make sense of exactly what happened. As you attempt to fit the different pieces of your memories together, you begin to wonder if you heard a snap or cracking noise in your ankle as you fell.

The more you think about it, the more convinced you become that you did in fact hear a noise as you fell. And not just a thump as you hit the floor. It was definitely a sharp, cracking noise.

Well, that can't be good. Can it?

Welcome to the hospital. Please wait.

The car pulls up as close to the hospital entrance as possible and you manage to extract yourself from it, then start slowly hobbling your way through the door to the Accident and Emergency department.

As you gingerly make your way to the reception desk, you're somewhat relieved to see that there isn't a queue. However, you can't help noticing that there are a number of people already sitting in the waiting room chairs.

Actually, there seem to be quite a few of them.

Many of them look like they've been there a while; blank stares, eyes half-closed. Some of them look like they could well be fast asleep.

As you (finally!) make it all the way over to the reception desk ("WHY do they not put them nearer the door?" you wonder), you're grateful to be able to lean on the counter and take the weight off your left leg once more.

You're in pain.

You're still recovering from the shock of the fall.

All you want is to get seen and treated as soon as possible, to be out of pain and back to normal again.

Is that too much to ask?

So, what happens now?

Before anything else happens, the receptionist will need to book you in.

They'll take a few details, like your name, address and contact number. They may also ask who your GP is. And then (*finally!*) they will ask why you are here.

After that, you will probably be asked to take a seat and wait to be called.

As you hop your way across to the nearest chair, you take the opportunity to have another look at the people already sitting in the waiting room.

You quickly realise that you might be in for a bit of a wait.

Sigh.

You can see a young man pressing an ice pack to his head. An older lady is sitting tenderly supporting her wrist, which looks a quite unusual shape. Nearly everybody is staring into space, seemingly resigned to the wait-of-unknown-length until they are seen.

Assessment

By necessity, hospitals have structured, well-planned systems in place to help them prioritise the people they see and treat. This is known as triage.

As a deliberately extreme example to show how this works in practice, a person suffering a heart attack or stroke will understandably need to be seen much more quickly than somebody who has merely stubbed their toe.

Life-threatening emergencies will <u>always</u> jump to the top of the priority scale.

The medical professionals in the hospital will use the information taken by the receptionist during your check-in process and then use their expertise, experience and clinical judgement, as well as certain "best practice" protocols, to triage people quickly and effectively.

This is all a *process.*

It is deliberate.

Planned by experts.

Reviewed regularly.

Updated as necessary.

Streamlined for maximum efficiency.

But it is (and always will be) a *process.*

(Remember this because we'll be thinking about *processes* quite a bit in this book.)

In the UK, when you visit an Accident and Emergency department you will often be seen first by an A&E nurse.

They will talk with you further about your problem and any symptoms you have. They'll normally ask about your previous medical history and whether you are on any medication.

A&E nurses are usually very experienced, and their role in seeing you is to narrow down a potential diagnosis. In your case, with your painful ankle, they may also arrange for you to have an X-ray to see if anything has broken.

Diagnosis

Once the nurse has seen you, you will probably have another wait before you are seen by an A&E doctor. At this point, they may well have a preliminary diagnosis in mind.

They will talk with you about your symptoms and review what the nurse previously discussed with you – often going through the same questions about your symptoms and whether you are currently on any medication.

Although at first this may look like a very inefficient way of assessing people, this deliberate duplication between the nurse and doctor is all part of a pre-planned *process* (there's that word again!) to ensure nothing gets missed or overlooked at any stage.

Assuming you've already had an X-ray of your ankle, previously arranged by the nurse, the doctor may now be able to give you an accurate diagnosis of the problem.

Unfortunately, it turns out that you have broken your ankle (well, the lower end of the tibia – one of the bones in your lower leg that help form the ankle joint).

<u>Again, please don't panic – this is only an imaginary story!</u>

(What kind of marketing book has you imagining you've broken your ankle? You wouldn't get this kind of thing in a book called "**How To Be A Marketing Ninja And Go From Zero To £1 Million In Under A Year**"...)

Treatment

It is important to realise that you will only receive treatment once a diagnosis has been made.

If you had hobbled into the hospital and immediately been directed onto a hospital bed, then wheeled through the corridors directly into an operating theatre, where the anaesthetist strapped a mask to your face as the surgical team waited to operate on your ankle...how would you have felt?

Alternatively, if you'd spoken to the nurse about your ankle pain and they had then started examining your eyes or testing your hearing...would you have felt confident in their ability to help you?

I hope your answer to the two questions above would be an emphatic "**NO**"!

You would obviously want the person in charge of your treatment to know exactly *what* they were treating. This can <u>only</u> come after a thorough investigation, looking at your symptoms and the results of any diagnostic tests, to make a diagnosis.

Remember, diagnosis first. Treatment second. If you get those the wrong way around, you'll quickly be in trouble (and in pain for longer).

Recovery

Once a diagnosis has been made and treatment has been planned, somebody will explain the recovery process to you, letting you know what to expect.

You may need to use crutches for a while, or to have your ankle stabilised by bandages or plaster. Because you needed surgery on your ankle, physiotherapy will be a must to ensure you regain as much strength, function and range of movement as possible.

Here's the most important point to remember - recovery is an essential part of the healing process.

If you try to *rush* your recovery, you may end up causing more extensive, longer-lasting (and harder-to-treat) damage to your ankle.

What does this have to do with business?

While this entire story has been imaginary, I wanted to walk you clearly through each part of the "medical emergency" process for a very specific reason.

The different stages of your medical journey – **injury, assessment, diagnosis, treatment, recovery** – are the same ones we are going to use as we explore your business and marketing throughout the rest of this book.

By applying these different stages to a business, you'll be able to see the correct *process* you need to go through to ensure healthy marketing and a healthy business.

Each step is very deliberate and needs to be worked through in the correct order. Can you imagine how chaotic healthcare would be if these stages were carried out in a different order? For example:

1. **Recovery**
2. **Treatment**
3. **Diagnosis**
4. **Assessment**
5. **Injury**

That order would be absurd in healthcare, yet similarly confused processes (and even *more* confused ones!) exist in many marketing departments around the world, as we shall see later in this book.

As you read this book, you will notice the very clear (and very deliberate) parallels between healthcare and the health of your business. I know that the metaphor is an imperfect one, but I have chosen to use it in order to make my points more memorable.

By using the healthcare framework and applying it to business, we'll (hopefully!) be able to see how to improve business health.

With that, an important caveat: I do not expect you to agree with everything said in this book. As the old saying goes, if we both agreed on everything, one of us would be unnecessary.

So, feel free to disagree with me if you'd like. I will not take it personally. (And as I said at the very beginning of this book, I am most definitely *not* a marketing guru whose every word is infallible.)

Agree with me or disagree with me, it's all okay.

But…my hope is that as you read this book, you will be able to think about marketing and business in a different way.

A better way.

A *healthier* way.

So, let's find out what exactly is meant by *healthy marketing*.

Chapter Two – What is Healthy Marketing?

So far in this book, you've read about our son's childhood leukaemia and have been asked to imagine falling down your stairs and injuring your ankle badly enough to require a hospital visit.

I'm guessing that you weren't expecting either of these things in a book supposedly about marketing!

If this was a regular marketing book, you might have been expecting me to regale you with a story about a mysterious (and always unnamed) business friend, who implemented the principles described in this book and went from £100,000 of debt to having a trillion pounds in the bank – in just 6 easy steps!

Similarly, if this was a standard health or fitness book (the kind often ghost-written for a celebrity and predominantly found in airport shops), this chapter would start off by showing you the classic 'before' and 'after' photos of me.

The first photo would show me looking more like a large potato than a human, while the second "after-following-the-exercise-programme-described-in-this-book" photo would show an *incredible* transformation; chiselled abs, tightly defined leg muscles, tanned body (why do those 'after' photos always need the person to be tanned?!)…and of course the obligatory new, much shorter haircut and far better lighting!

(The slightly worrying thing is that if I did in fact use stories like these, there are probably some people who would read them and accept them as true. How else do you think many supposed 'marketing experts' make their money?)

So, for complete transparency, I am *not* taking that approach.

While there is certainly a place for such transformational stories in the overall context of a balanced marketing campaign, I believe that the sheer extent of many of these transformations can make them seem unbelievable, out of the reach of a normal person.

I want this book to be helpful to 'ordinary' people, so I'll be keeping everything simple enough that even I can understand it.

(Whether I'm copywriting or marketing, training or teaching, I always work on the principle that if I can understand something, *anybody* can!)

Defining our terms

Before attempting to change any aspect of business or marketing, it's important to know what exactly we're looking to improve or achieve as a result. (Remember the importance of an accurate diagnosis in the last chapter?)

Change for the sake of change is often nothing but foolishness.

As part of my degree, I had to learn the different parts of every bone in the human body so that I could describe them accurately to a doctor if necessary.

Post-graduation, when working in hospital, I quickly became fluent in medical terminology, taking words and phrases like 'ORIF' (open reduction, internal fixation), 'DHS' (dynamic hip screw) and 'FOOSH' (fall onto outstretched hand) in my stride.

My wife trained as a pharmacist, so can you imagine the conversations we used to have with one another over an evening meal? (This was pre-children, when we could both still string two words together…)

As medically minded as much of our conversations were, we made it up to our friends by being pretty useful with the medical questions in quizzes or crosswords.

<u>Defining terms correctly is just as important for marketers as it is for medical doctors.</u>

Unfortunately, many marketers – particularly, but not exclusively, those relying on online media – seem to be shockingly happy to use poorly-defined phrases in their attempt to justify badly-conceived goals executed ineffectively.

This may of course be down to the fact that many of the 'solutions' they offer do not lend themselves to any form of accountability or accurate measurement.

By failing to define terms, they can then pick and choose what to measure – which surprisingly always seems to show them in an extremely good light!

To avoid such subterfuge, con artistry and outright deception (can you tell what I *really* think about many marketing and ad agencies?), let's actually define our terms.

Before we start thinking further about *healthy marketing*, it's helpful to clarify what exactly we mean by both 'healthy' and 'marketing'.

Health (and Fitness)

The dictionary has a few definitions of health that match nicely (*almost as though I planned it this way…!*) with the main thrust of this book:

- 'The state of being free from illness or injury'
- 'A person's mental or physical condition'

Using these as a guide, we could simply say that a healthy person is one who is free from illness or injury.

But does that tell the whole story?

Is the *absence* of illness or injury the only criteria we should use to determine health?

Or is that only a small part of what constitutes health?

Several years ago, I watched a promotional video on YouTube for CrossFit®, the company that popularised functional fitness. The video was titled '**A Test of Fitness**' and I thoroughly recommend watching it if you can find it online. It's entertaining, informative and fascinating to watch, particularly if you are interested in health and fitness.

As somebody who has loved health and fitness for many years, I found myself embarrassingly stumped by a question that was asked in that video – **how do you define fitness**?

Such a simple question, yet one I found myself struggling to answer.

Is the 'fittest' person the strongest person?

The fastest?

The most flexible?

The one who can jump the highest or throw something the furthest distance?

The one with the greatest endurance?

The point made in the video was that fitness is a combination of many different aspects.

If you focus exclusively on one aspect of fitness, you will only be 'fit' in that one area.

If you mix all the different components together - strength, flexibility, speed, endurance, stamina, etc. – somewhere in the mix will be the perfect blend.

Now while that video was intended primarily to promote the philosophy and benefits of CrossFit®, I've found that it's helpful to use the same approach when thinking about marketing and business.

Never skip leg day

A professional bodybuilder who focuses on the size of their biceps while neglecting their legs will look unbalanced and out of proportion. Hence the well-known saying to *never skip leg day.*

For what it's worth, such a person is also highly unlikely to be a world-leading marathon runner. (Or an Olympic-level gymnast for that matter.)

In the same way, a business that is relying on one aspect of marketing but completely neglecting others is unlikely to be successful (however you choose to define 'success'), particularly over the longer-term.

Marketing strategist Jay Abraham refers to this as being the difference between your business being like a diving board or the Parthenon.

A diving board, with just one supporting pillar, will collapse if that pillar is removed. If one support in the Parthenon is removed, the structure will remain standing.

Which would be the healthier type of business to have - a diving board or Parthenon-based one?

Marketing

What *is* marketing? And is it even important nowadays?

With an increasingly online, digital world, in which we're told that people are developing ever-shorter attention spans, do we even need marketing anymore?

A traditional description of marketing would say that it's about promoting or advertising a product or service, of raising awareness, of helping to sell something.

While this is a good starting point, it's also quite vague. What exactly does it *mean*? And how can you tell if your marketing is working?

I prefer a much broader approach to describing marketing, for marketing is not just a department or a job title. I believe that marketing is *everything* in your business.

Whether it's the way a receptionist answers the phone or the appearance of your website and how easy it is to navigate, how quickly you reply to an enquiry or the quality of the products or services you offer, *everything* is marketing.

Effective, *healthy* marketing means that all the different elements of your business are working together to communicate the same message.

That means that marketing is not dependent only on people whose job title describes them as marketers. *Everybody* working in the company – whether cleaner or CEO, salesperson or receptionist – plays a vital role in marketing. (And sales, but that's for another book.)

If we approach marketing using the framework of health, we can see many similarities to the human body. Every part of your body, no matter how big or small, plays an important role in the body working properly.

If you've ever stubbed a toe or caught a finger in a door, you'll know just how painful and limiting even quite a small part of the body can be when it is damaged or dysfunctional.

When something more significant is damaged or not working properly, for example following a heart attack or hip fracture, it may cause pain and limit your movement and activity for a long time.

It would be ridiculous to claim that a person who is in hospital for coronary artery bypass graft surgery is healthy because their *eyesight* is good.

Even if they have 20/20 vision, the fact they're having heart surgery suggests that *something* isn't working properly in their body!

It would be similarly ridiculous to say that a business with a good lead generation process, but poor conversion, sales and follow-up processes is a completely healthy one.

Either the whole business is healthy or none of it is.

Blood and business

As blood is pumped through your body, it delivers oxygen and essential nutrients and removes waste products.

If anything blocks the normal flow of blood, such as occurs when a clot develops in a blood vessel, it will end up causing damage to the body.

If we think of marketing in the same way, essential for every part of a business, we can see that anything that prevents marketing working as it normally does may end up causing damage to the business.

(As with the other healthcare and body-based metaphors used in this book, this is an imperfect one. Nonetheless,

it helps us to think about marketing a little bit differently than a standard business book.)

The Perfect 'Fit'

Much as a healthy body is one that can function properly, without pain, stiffness, disease or damage, a healthy business is one in which all the different parts and processes – manufacturing, distribution, marketing, sales, aftercare, admin etc. – are functioning properly and working together smoothly, effectively and without 'pain' at any point.

If we take things a step further, we can see the clear link in the human body between 'health' and 'fitness'.

Generally, if you improve your fitness, you will improve your health. Strength, flexibility, endurance and recovery all play an important role in fitness and health.

Similarly, a fit and healthy business is one that not only functions properly but is one that is strong, flexible, resilient and built to last.

As the subtitle to this book proclaims on the front cover:

Better marketing health
Greater business *wealth*

Of course, knowledge of this is only a small part of a much bigger picture. Knowledge is absolutely useless in isolation. It is only when the knowledge about a health concern is acted upon that anything can begin to improve.

As Dale Carnegie (and many others) said:

Knowledge is not power until it's *applied*.

Said another way, knowledge is only *potential* power. *Action* is power.

So healthy marketing is best described as being marketing that permits and facilitates all the different parts and processes of a business to work together for one (and only one) common purpose – to generate a profit.

If you don't like or agree with that definition, it's no problem. Many people feel uneasy about the thought of making a profit, particularly when that aim is stated so boldly. But that *is* the definition I'm using and the one that will permeate through the rest of this book.

The unhealthy alternative

Now that we have a bit more of an idea what healthy marketing is, we're going to flip things around and have a look at what happens to a business when things *aren't* as healthy as they should be.

That's right! In chapter three, we're going to take a close look at 'marketing gone bad,' so that we can easily detect the common symptoms of unhealthy marketing.

Unfortunately, you'll soon discover that finding unhealthy, diseased marketing is all too easy nowadays. You really don't have to go far to find it!

So, without further ado, let's jump into the mess that is much of modern marketing.

Brace yourself and hold your nose to avoid the stench – things are about to get decidedly mucky in the next chapter!

Chapter Three – Symptoms

Most of us will only choose to see a doctor or other health professional when we have a specific health issue or because of certain symptoms that are causing us concern.

Often, the type and location of our symptoms will help to narrow down possible causes, but this is not always the case.

(For example, our son's leg pain pre-diagnosis could have easily been mistaken for cramp or 'growing pains'. A GP thought it might be arthritic flu. Leukaemia wasn't even on our radar.)

Other people will seek medical help because they have a pre-existing medical condition that requires regular monitoring and assessment.

Other than these reasons, or to get certain vaccines needed for travel or a health check for insurance purposes, it is rare for somebody to access medical help when they have no symptoms, no health concerns or no pre-existing conditions.

Healthy or not?

Similarly, it is easy for a business with no obvious 'symptoms' of poor health to carry on as normal, assuming that everything is okay. In the absence of any obvious problems, as long as the clients keep coming and money continues to come in, everything can appear healthy, particularly if only looked at on a superficial level.

While such a business may in fact be healthy, a *smart* business owner or marketer will still keep a very close eye indeed on certain aspects of their business.

They know that a problem in any area of the business could be an early warning indicator of a potential issue in the future.

By looking out for these early warnings, a smart marketer or business owner can take action quickly to (hopefully) prevent a problem growing and developing into a larger, more damaging one.

In the weeks leading up to our son's diagnosis of leukaemia, he had various symptoms like unusual fatigue, pain in a foot, pale skin.

We were aware of these symptoms and did all that we could to help alleviate them.

We hugged him, rubbed his feet, gave him paracetamol – all the things parents do when their child is unhappy and in pain.

We were in and out of our local GP surgery a number of times, where we listened to their advice and followed their suggestions.

But…we didn't stop and look at all of the seemingly separate symptoms and put them together. We were so busy trying to manage the symptoms, we were not able to step back and look at the bigger picture.

It was only when we took him directly from yet another GP appointment to the A&E department of Bristol Children's Hospital that this bigger picture became clearer.

As we talked with the hospital staff and went through a very similar triage process to the one described in Chapter One, all the different symptoms began to be looked at as part of the same underlying problem.

The very first nurse we saw at the hospital told us that her alarm bells were ringing from the medical history we had given.

Our son's assessment was bumped up to a different priority level and certain tests were carried out as part of their pre-planned, well-oiled process to get to a firm diagnosis as quickly as possible.

Left to our own devices, my wife and I would have continued trying to help our son as we had been – hugs, paracetamol, prayer, despair.

Who knows how long we would have carried on doing those things for? We *thought* we were doing the right things (and we were in, as much as we knew then).

We'd sought advice from the GP, from the 111 telephone helpline and from an out-of-hours GP appointment over the weekend.

But none of these things were ever going to be able to effectively treat his leukaemia. The only way his type of leukaemia could be treated was with intensive, aggressive chemotherapy.

(Sigh.)

We don't know how long the leukaemia had been developing inside our son's bone marrow. It was only when his symptoms became more pronounced that we realised something was wrong and that expert help was needed.

It was only when we were in the right place (the hospital) and with the right people (the Oncology team) that we were able to get an accurate diagnosis.

Knowing what we now know, if the same thing happened again, we would take him directly to the hospital for assessment by the Oncology team.

In fact, as I'm writing this chapter, we had to do exactly this just a few weeks ago, when he had symptoms that could potentially have been a sign of relapse (i.e. the leukaemia returning). We were <u>incredibly</u> grateful when a full examination by the A&E team followed by the all-important blood test gave him the all-clear.

Phew.

Even though we had fairly quick confirmation that the leukaemia had not returned, my wife and I still had a few days of worry as we recalled just how hard and draining his treatment had been on us all as a family.

The difference between pre-leukaemia and now is that we *know* the symptoms to look out for. We *know* that the fastest way to properly assess things is with a blood test at the hospital. We *know* the people we need to see.

The Oncology team have repeatedly told us to go directly to the hospital if we have any concerns about relapse.

That's what they are there for (and we are very grateful for them!).

In case you've been reading the above thinking it was *only* about our son's leukaemia, please think again. I'm sharing this story with you to make a deliberate point:

Isn't this a lot like business?

Hmmmm.

As business owners, as marketers, it can be SO easy to just carry on doing what we *think* is best for our business.

If any problems occur, we try to resolve them *reactively*, as they happen, rather than *proactively* in advance.

Perhaps we always try to 'fix' problems the same way we always have, never looking to see if there's a better way, or some way that we can prevent this problem occurring again.

<u>It is often only when we step back and look at the bigger picture that we can see the true extent of any problems.</u>

Sometimes we might need an outside expert to come in and help us to *see* this bigger picture (*although be careful which highly paid business consultant you get in to help you, and ALWAYS keep a close eye on what they're billing you for!*).

So let me ask you a question:

When did you last step back and look at your business in its entirety?

Have you *ever* stepped back, or are you so busy putting out fires, chasing new business and trying to keep all the plates spinning, that you haven't got the time to stop, step back and take a holistic look at your business as a whole?

Mild or severe?

In our bodies, symptoms caused by illness, disease or trauma can range from mild through to severe. The severity of the symptoms will often (but not always) be a good indicator of the seriousness of the problem and may help to inform the type of treatment needed.

By way of example, let's imagine a person who is suffering with arthritis in the hip. Specifically, we'll use osteoarthritis, the most common type of arthritis in the UK. (I've also chosen it because I have written so many pages of content for clients about this condition over the years that I know a little bit about it!)

Osteoarthritis causes the smooth lining on the ends of bones (the *articular cartilage*) to break down more rapidly than normal.

In a healthy joint, as the bones move against one another, the articular cartilage helps ensure movement is smooth and free of friction. As osteoarthritis develops in a joint and the articular cartilage is broken down more, movement of the bones against one another starts to cause friction. This friction leads to pain and stiffness in the joint.

In the earlier stages of osteoarthritis, there may be no symptoms to notice. If there *is* any pain or stiffness, it will often be relatively mild and is usually thought of as being a natural part of ageing.

As osteoarthritis progresses and the cartilage is broken down more extensively, the symptoms become much more pronounced, eventually causing severe pain and stiffness in the joint.

A person with advanced osteoarthritis in their hip may be extremely slow and limited in their movements, having to rely on a mobility aid to move themselves safely. They will often also be in pain a lot of the time.

Despite the effect such a condition has on daily life, many people with osteoarthritis in their hip will not seek any type of medical guidance or help until their symptoms become too severe to ignore.

By this stage, they may well have been struggling for weeks, months or even years with pain and stiffness in their hip.

Other people may seek medical advice at a much earlier stage, while symptoms are still relatively mild. In these cases, a physiotherapist or an osteopath may be able to help relieve or manage the symptoms.

Here's the key point - somebody with mild symptoms would not expect to be told by their doctor that they need total hip replacement surgery immediately!

If you went to see a doctor about mild hip pain and they asked you to get up onto their consulting table so that they could operate on you immediately, you would hopefully ignore their advice (and run out of the consulting room as quickly as possible!).

Ridiculous in healthcare, just another day for a marketer

Even though such a scenario seems so ridiculous to us, isn't this precisely the type of thing that happens in business every day?

If you've ever approached a marketing agency or copywriter for help, you may have been surprised at how quickly they tried to 'operate' on you to remove money from your business and deposit it into their own (I like to refer to such a treatment as a '*budget-ectomy*' or '*financial transfusion*'!).

Without taking the time to assess your particular symptoms, or to find out more about your business and industry, they will often want to jump straight into selling you their products or services (i.e. *treatments*) that may or may not be the right ones for you.

Just as some medical doctors like to use long words to make themselves look clever, many marketers will try to use phrases or buzzwords to confuse and intimidate people into hiring them.

Words and phrases like 'SEO', 'content marketing', 'blogs', 'social media', 'likes', 'views' and 'shares'.

While such a person will often pat themselves on the back when they successfully fool (a.k.a 'sell' something to) a person using this approach, they delude only themselves if they think this is an ethical, *healthy* way to run a business.

If you need to confuse somebody in order to sell them something, the chances are high that what you are selling is not providing any value to them.

So what other danger signs do we need to be aware of in our business?

How can we tell if we need expert 'treatment' for a problem?

Do some problems resolve themselves if left alone?

What can we do to make sure we don't fall for some kind of marketing scam that may end up causing serious, possibly *permanent* damage to our business?

Do you have any of these common symptoms?

There are clear symptoms of unhealthy marketing and of an unhealthy business.

The earlier you are aware of any symptoms, the sooner you will be able to treat the underlying cause(s) and prevent more extensive (possibly fatal) damage to your business.

As somebody who likes to think differently, I must apologise in advance for what you are about to read.

Given the 'healthy' approach to business I've chosen to take in this book, I have decided to cleverly (or, more likely, purely for my own amusement) merge some common health problems with well-known business and marketing topics to make them memorable - and to hopefully make you smile.

You'll very quickly see that many of them have been crowbarred in, very inelegantly. Alliteration is used with abandon (and with no shame!).

[Continue reading at your own risk -
you have been warned!]

Symptoms and conditions of unhealthy marketing or an unhealthy business include:

- *Follow-Up Fever*
- *Sales Sweats*
- *Phone Call Phobia*
- *Advertising Angina*
- *Lead Lethargy*
- *Brand Bursitis*

- *Inbound Marketing Irritation*
- *Persuasion-induced Palpitations*
- *Marketing Migraines*
- *Hard Work Headaches*
- *Meeting Meningitis*
- *Ad Words Amputation*
- *SEO Short-Sightedness*
- *Campaign Colitis*
- *Arthritic Algorithms*
- *Pale Profits*
- *Anaemic Advertising*
- *Budget Bloat*
- *Retargeting Reflux*
- *Spreadsheet Soreness*
- *A/B Testing Addiction*
- *PDF Parasite*
- *Dynamic Content Depression*
- *Tracking Tics*
- *Financial Fibrillation*
- *Backend Blindness*
- *Content Marketing Confusion*
- *Upsell Ulcer*
- *Infographic Infection*
- *Bounce Rate Burnout*
- *Call-to-action Confusion*
- *Social Media Stiffness*
- *Pay-Per-Click Pain*
- *ROI Rash*

- *Webform Weakness*
- *GDPR Gout*

Although the list above was written with my tongue firmly in my cheek, there is (sadly!) a lot of truth contained within it as well.

If you have been involved in marketing for years, you may have found yourself with a wry smile on your face as you read through the list.

If you're *new* to marketing, you may have recognised a few of these terms from what you've seen online or read in a regular marketing book.

Either way, all the symptoms mentioned above will often be caused by something unhealthy in the marketing itself, or the business.

When symptoms are discovered, my approach is always to take a step back, look at the bigger picture and ask myself:

- What could be causing this symptom?

- Have I seen this symptom before? If so, how did I treat it then?

- In what way(s) is this symptom impacting my ability to make a profit?

- If left untreated, how will this symptom develop?

- Are there any other symptoms in the business that may be linked to this one?

- How can I treat this symptom so that it doesn't come back?

The Problem With Symptoms

I've been fortunate to have run the London Marathon a couple of times.

More recently, I've completed ultramarathons* of 100 kilometres, raising money for CLIC Sargent, a charity supporting children with cancer. (They were a huge help to us all as a family during our son's treatment, so it was a privilege to be able to raise some money for them.)

**You'll read more about these later in this book.*

In short, I love fitness and am a keen proponent of improving our health.

I am a firm believer that if most people exercised more - not necessarily pumping heavy weights in the gym, but just taking some gentle exercise like going for a walk every day - they would be much healthier.

(The added advantage of this would be reduced pressures on the health service in this country over time, but that's one for the politicians to argue over…)

However, the <u>reality</u> is that many people do not choose to make fitness or health a priority.

There are a lot of *unhealthy* people.

There are a lot of people who eat *unhealthy* things.

There are a lot of people *choosing* to put unhealthy things into their bodies every day.

In the Western world, certain illnesses, diseases and medical conditions – like cancer, diabetes and obesity - are on the increase.

Unfortunately, no matter how much money is pumped into health awareness initiatives or healthy eating, no matter how much tax is added to sugar, there will always be some people who choose to stay with an unhealthy diet and lifestyle.

(Please know that this is not intended to be a judgement on them. I fully appreciate many people are extremely

limited with their budget for food, what they know about nutrition and healthy eating etc.- I am using this as an example purely to emphasise a point.)

And of course, many people are unhealthy without really knowing it.

Somebody who is just starting to experience the very first signs or symptoms of cancer may have had the cancer growing in their body for a while before the symptoms developed enough for them to notice (just like with our son).

Other people will *know* that they are not fit, that they are not healthy, that their lifestyle and diet is not healthy. But the thought of change is just too much for them to consider.

**As an aside, if you are interested in discovering more about the psychology of change, I highly recommend the book 'Change Or Die' by Alan Deutschman.*

And so they *choose* to remain in their unhealthy state. Over time, this unhealthy lifestyle increases the risk of them developing certain serious illnesses.

The same can be said of businesses around the world.

There are some businesses that are choosing to market in a healthy way. They are approaching their marketing sustainably, sensibly, strategically, wisely, efficiently and effectively. They have a long-term approach. They are keeping the good stuff 'in' and the bad stuff, the unhealthy stuff 'out'.

By the same token, many businesses around the world are incredibly unhealthy in how they choose to market themselves and in how they choose to operate. Their focus is often exceptionally short-term results.

This may be due to the way they were set up, how they are structured, the ways they have chosen to market themselves or the way they move money into and out of the business.

If your business is unhealthy, over time you will begin to see warning signs. They may be mild warning signs or more serious ones.

- They may show up as **reduced profits** or a **higher turnover of clients**.

- Perhaps the customers you *do* have are spending less than they used to.

- You may find yourself **having to work harder** to get new clients or to make a sale.

- Maybe you start <u>getting less than ideal clients</u>, who take up more of your time, are more demanding and unwilling to pay your normal rates.

- Are you finding it **harder to attract or to keep good staff**?

- Does keeping the business going just seem so much *harder* than it used to?

All of these are good indicators that something is unhealthy in your business. Some part or process is not working properly, and that is causing problems in the business.

Shortly in this book, we will be looking at how to diagnose a problem in your business if you notice any unhealthy symptoms.

Before we start diagnosing anything though, I'd like to invite you to travel back in time to 1998 and join me at the London Marathon.

So lace up your imaginary running shoes, stretch those calves and prepare to start jogging.

Things are about to get…interesting!

Chapter Four - My Hydration Mistake

I count myself as fortunate to have run the London Marathon twice. Both times were when I was much younger, and it was a bit easier to get a place than it is today.

I'm going to share a story with you about the second time I ran it. It involves my lovely sister, who will probably kill me if she ever reads this book (which is unlikely – as a primary school teacher, I'm not sure she's ever going to be interested in healthy marketing!).

We were both in our twenties and were lined up in Blackheath about to start the London Marathon. We had both been training for a while, my sister had new running shoes and we were READY!

As I had run it a couple of years previously, I decided to gracefully bestow some pearls of wisdom upon my sister. After all, I had completed it last time in under 4 hours. Therefore, I was now an expert on *everything* to do with marathon running.

(Sigh. The arrogance of youth.)

It was a fairly warm day, so I emphasised to her the importance of staying hydrated. “Don’t wait until you feel thirsty to drink, because you’ll already be dehydrated by that stage,” I proclaimed.

My sister listened to my advice.

For reasons you will discover shortly, I really hope that the advice in this book is more helpful to you than the advice I gave to my sister was…

BANG! And We’re Off.

The race started and we began moving slowly along with the thousands of other runners, just 26.2 miles to go until we reached the finish!

Now the London Marathon at the time had water stations located every mile. On a number of tables either side of the route were hundreds of small bottles of water, available to grab and drink if you needed to.

I was running at a different pace to my sister, so hoped she remembered my advice about drinking plenty.

Unfortunately, she did!

Determined to avoid dehydration, she picked up a water bottle every mile and drank it.

Yep - she went around the entire 26.2-mile route drinking a bottle of water every mile.

Come to think of it, I'm not sure whether she ran or sloshed her way around the route…

When we met up afterwards, I found out that she'd had so much water she had needed to stop to visit the portable toilets on the route SIX TIMES!!

Now when you have thousands of runners involved, you get a lot of people needing to visit the portable toilets during the course of a marathon. With far fewer toilets than runners needing them, queues soon form.

My poor sister ended up queuing at each of the six portable toilets she stopped at. We think this added at least an **hour** on to her marathon time!

She was doing it to raise money for charity and was thrilled to have finished. She had done a great job and was rightly proud of her achievement.

As her younger brother, I couldn't help but feel pretty bad that my advice about keeping hydrated had not been a little bit more nuanced.

If I'd been clearer with my suggestion about drinking regularly, sipping water frequently but NOT drinking a bottle every mile, she would have finished at least an hour sooner.

(Mind you, we did laugh a lot about that as a family. Even now, many years after it happened, I've been chuckling to myself as I've been writing this chapter and remembering that day!)

Why have I told you this story about "**My Sister And Her Quest For The Portable Toilet"**?

What on earth can this possibly have to do with marketing or business?

Pacing yourself

It's very easy to read a marketing book (like this one!) or to hear a talk by a marketer you respect and to get overly enthusiastic about any advice they give. It is all too easy to rush into things too quickly, without pausing to consider adjusting the pace of any changes you're going to make.

Whenever you hear *anything* from a business leader, marketer or training consultant, always run it through your common-sense filter. Ask yourself questions like:

- Does what they are saying make sense?

- Does it sound too good to be true?

- If I did the <u>opposite</u> of what they're telling me to do, what might happen?

- *Why* are they telling me this? Is it so that they can sell something to me?

- Why should I listen to them? Do they have personal experience in this area?

While it is important to always be learning new things, growing and developing, it is even more important to choose who you listen to very carefully.

As the old saying goes:

All that glitters is not gold

Just like my incredibly hydrated sister running the London Marathon thought that she was using the advice I had given her properly, it can be easy to learn some new tactic or approach and then to overuse it, or to introduce it too quickly into your business.

And just like my sister, you may end up slowing yourself down as a result.

If you have an imbalance, it may dilute (*see what I did there?)* the effectiveness of your marketing.

By way of example, let's imagine that you are a business owner who has not previously run any type of ad on Facebook®.

You (hopefully) wouldn't decide to suddenly spend £20,000 a month on running these types of ads just because a friend of yours told you that you should.

Rather, you would look further into the possibility of running these ads.

You would talk to other people who are experts in that area to find out what you should do.

If you rush into doing something without proper analysis, you will usually end up regretting it.

Even though this book has been written to help you, I cannot emphasise enough that the information and ideas you read in these pages need to be balanced.

Despite what many marketers will tell you (usually for a hefty fee!), there is <u>not</u> a one-size-fits-all approach to marketing.

As I said at the very beginning of this book, I am *not* a guru. I do *not* have all the answers. All I can do is offer you a new way of thinking. Always assess what I say in this book. Weigh it up against what *you* know and how *you* think about business.

Then use the bits that work for you and ignore those that don't.

It's good to have an open mind, but not one that is *so* open your brains fall out.

Finish Sooner

Despite following my advice to stay hydrated a little bit too literally, my sister finished the London Marathon. She got to the end and received her medal.

She would have finished much sooner if she hadn't taken my advice quite so literally.

As you continue reading this book, please take the time to assess the ideas and thoughts within. Do not assume that everything I say is going to work for every business 100% of the time.

That just isn't realistic.

Incidentally, this is one of the main reasons I am giving a framework in this book, a way of thinking about marketing, rather than a step-by-step “**Ultimate Guide to Marketing Success**”!

So, I think you’ve now heard enough about my sister and her incredible ability to overhydrate during a marathon.

After this brief detour, let’s get back into marketing mode by looking in the next chapter at how to diagnose a marketing problem.

Chapter Five - Diagnosis

Over the years, I have worked with and spoken to *hundreds* of medical consultants.

While working as a diagnostic radiographer, I spent countless hours in operating theatres, providing imaging for orthopaedic and urological surgeons.

I worked many hundreds of hours in A&E, on both day and night shifts, providing X-ray imaging for a wide variety of injuries and conditions.

My time working as a medical sales representative involved meeting with medical doctors, talking with them about certain conditions and treatment options.

As a copywriter, I have spent many (*many*!) hours talking with medical consultants on the phone and via Zoom®, interviewing them for various content marketing projects I've been hired to work on.

Without fail, every single medical consultant, every medical doctor, every nurse, every physiotherapist, *anybody* who is involved in the medical field would (or *should*) tell you that the most important step to receiving the optimal treatment for your condition is to first get an accurate diagnosis.

Before planning treatment, you need to know what is causing your symptoms

Sometimes, a diagnosis may be relatively straightforward and quick to make.

For example, it may be fairly obvious that somebody has a fractured wrist (or more commonly, a fracture in the lower part of their *radius* or *ulna*, the bones of the forearm) because their wrist has a certain unusual shape to it.

Often, it will be the shape of a dinner fork, with a bend near the wrist where there really should not be a bend. An X-ray of their wrist would show the fracture(s), confirming the diagnosis so that treatment could be planned.

In other cases, diagnosis may be far more complex, requiring several investigations and tests before an accurate diagnosis can be confirmed.

For example, somebody struggling with fibromyalgia or chronic fatigue syndrome will often have a number of different symptoms with many possible causes.

Over time, appropriate investigations are used to exclude certain causes in order to narrow down a diagnosis.

The unhealthy realities of *misdiagnosis*

Before we look any further at making an accurate diagnosis, let's look at the dangers of *misdiagnosis*.

An online search showed me that successful claims made for wrong diagnosis cost the NHS £12.2 million between 2014 – 2015.

£12.2 *million*.

Not only is that financially shocking, it is of course a sobering reminder that people's lives would have been significantly affected by a misdiagnosis.

To further hammer this point home, a Mayo Clinic study revealed that only 12% of patients seeking second opinions from the Mayo Clinic had been correctly diagnosed by their primary care providers. More than 20% had been misdiagnosed, while 66% required some changes to their initial diagnosis.

How scary is that?

20% had been misdiagnosed and 66% needed some changes to their initial diagnosis.

How much anxiety or worry would the affected patients have experienced as a result of their misdiagnosis? How can you put a price on it?

There is also the awareness that when a diagnosis is made later, treatment may be more challenging or less effective if the disease has spread.

Misdiagnosis is *bad.*

Misdiagnosis is *dangerous*.

Misdiagnosis is *unhealthy*.

I'm sure you can see where I'm going with this because this of course has parallels with business. It is not enough just to say that something is wrong in your business.

The more important question is - **is your diagnosis accurate**? Is it *correct*?

- Who has made the diagnosis?
- What qualifies them to have made the diagnosis?
- Are they somebody that you should listen to? (Or somebody maybe you should be a bit wary of listening to?)

What do you need to make a diagnosis?

Making an accurate diagnosis depends on several different things. In healthcare terms, these might include:

- Symptoms
- Medical history
- Results of any investigations (X-rays, blood tests etc.)
- Clinical judgement

Doctors need to be (*but aren't always, in practice*!) extremely good at listening carefully to their patients – not just for what they say, but also for what they *don't* say.

A patient may say something as an aside, but a doctor who is listening carefully will be able to use that one additional piece of information to help them determine what is causing the symptoms.

One of the occupational hazards of being a healthcare worker is that it can be very easy to fall into the trap of classifying people according to their symptoms. A person becomes thought of as "the knee patient", "the hip patient" or "the headache patient".

In my radiography days, we used to be told that we had "a wrist coming around for an X-ray" – almost forgetting that the wrist was attached firmly to a real person. An impersonal description; a problem to be solved rather than a person struggling with a health issue.

An alternative approach

Other doctors will take a holistic approach, looking at the person as a whole and not 'just' as a knee, a hip or a headache!

While somebody may visit a doctor complaining of knee pain, a holistic approach will recognise the varied effects that knee pain may be having on their quality of life. Certain activities may no longer be possible.

- Moving safely around the house might be difficult.

- A person may have to rely on somebody else to do their shopping for them.

- There may be frustration or anger that a favourite sport can no longer be played or enjoyed

- Disappointment that a grandparent is not able to bend down to play with a grandchild on the floor

- Waking at night due to the pain, then finding it hard to get back to sleep again

Hopefully, I've painted a vivid enough picture in your mind!

If a doctor focuses *only* on the physical problem in the knee, they risk missing the emotional and mental impact the knee pain is having on their patient.

<u>The same is true in business, where a singular focus on one specific area may cause you to overlook other important aspects or areas.</u>

For example, a business relying *purely* on Facebook® advertising to generate leads is missing out on advertising to anybody who isn't on that particular platform.

The company may be okay with that, but it *is* an issue. If Facebook® changes the algorithms it uses, or decides to change its Terms of Service and kicks the business off the platform without warning, how 'healthy' will that business be?

If a business focuses *only* on bringing in new customers, they run the risk of neglecting their current ones. By chasing the lure of 'new', they may lose the reliable income of their previous and repeat customers.

Services and Products or Client-Focused Results?

Much as a healthcare worker may start referring to patients as “the knee problem” or “the hip arthritis”, businesses can easily find themselves referring to their customers and clients as impersonal objects, rather than people in need of a particular result.

- The receptionist in a hair salon whose way of letting the hairdresser know their next client has arrived is to tell them, **“Your 10 o’clock is here!”**

- The dentist being told that “**the filling**” is in the waiting room

- The IT company discussing the “SEO client”

- The marketing agency referring to a client as “**suckers**”. (Sorry! I couldn’t resist having yet another dig at marketing agencies, could I?)

While it’s a cliché, it is also true that people buy a particular product or service for the *result* they expect to get from it.

A person buying a drill at the DIY store is (probably) not buying it purely because it looks like a beautiful drill, and they want to mount it on the living room wall for people to admire.

Nor are they buying it purely to drill holes into something.

They are buying it for what it will enable them to do once any holes have been drilled – for example, securely fixing a shelf to the wall (upon which they can store their spare copies of **The Healthy Marketing Handbook**…).

That's right. I'm promoting my own book inside my own book – which you *already* own.

"Is there no end to his self-promotion?" I hear you ask.

Erm, sorry - no!

When is a diagnosis needed?

If you've noticed symptoms in your business, such as a poor result from a recent marketing campaign, you will need to investigate the possible causes to arrive at a diagnosis.

You may be content to let any symptoms continue for a while, particularly if they're not causing significant problems in your business. If they are allowed to continue for a longer period - a month, three months, six months, 12 months – they have the potential for having a magnified effect on your business profits and future income.

Just as in a healthcare setting, it is important not to make a diagnosis too quickly. Before a diagnosis can be made, it's important you *properly* investigate the problem, examining it from all angles.

It is always worth investigating thoroughly, as an incorrect diagnosis may cause you to try to waste time and money treating the wrong thing.

How is a diagnosis made?

A hospital will have many diagnostic capabilities held within its walls, including blood tests, X-ray imaging, MRI scans, ultrasound and endoscopy. Each provides different types of diagnostic information.

For example, a CT scanner uses X-rays and computer technology to create cross-sectional images of the body. It provides much more detailed information than a standard (plain) X-ray can. MRI scans provide much more detail about the soft tissues.

In business, some problems may be simple to diagnose, while others will require more time and effort. Some may be relatively easy to fix, while others will run much deeper in the business and require extensive re-arrangement, remodelling and restructuring of the business to take it from failing to thriving; unprofitable to profitable; 'unhealthy' to 'healthy'.

Healthy marketing involves taking a comprehensive, all-encompassing *honest* look at your business – not just looking at what you *think* the problem might be.

You want to be looking at everything, including:

- Your business systems
- Your customers
- The results *you're* getting
- The results your *customers* are getting
- Changes in the lifetime value of your customers
- How customers are first coming to you (i.e. lead sources)
- Trends in your business and your industry – both current and future

- Trends in customer spending
- Cost of lead acquisition (and changes in this over time)
- Strengths and weaknesses in your business
- Strengths and weaknesses of your competition
- Referral pathways
- Current daily, weekly and monthly income – and changes in this over the previous 3, 6, 9, 12 months
- Your pricing strategies
- Your offers – are they working, which ones are getting the best results?

Depending on your specific business symptoms, you may want to take a further step back from your business and industry and look at:

- Political changes that may be affecting (or could affect) spending behaviours or economic forecasts

- Changes in popular culture

- Global tax changes, and their potential implications on your business

- Advances in technology – both where they impact on your business directly, or could be used in your business for better effectiveness

- Where money is moving FROM and TO (e.g. from offline to online, print to digital).

This sounds like a lot of work!

There's no denying that this all involves effort, energy and focus. In other words, **hard work** (two words not found in many business or marketing books!).

Most business owners and marketers prefer to avoid this type of hard work, focusing their efforts on finding the ONE 'quick fix' or 'hack' they need to turn things around.

They seek out the easy solution rather than the more complex one. Yet it is often the more complex approach that will provide the best, longer-lasting benefits.

Although this has already been said several times in this book, I will repeat it once more because it is so important:

An accurate diagnosis is crucial to getting the right treatment

The aim of making a diagnosis is to be able to focus treatment on the right area(s) of your business. The very worst thing you could do is to make a very quick diagnosis of what you *think* the problem is, then pour energy, time and money into fixing that problem, only to find out later that you were treating the wrong thing.

Diagnosis first. Treatment second.

** For a more detailed exploration of the movement of money, I highly recommend reading Dan Kennedy's 'Almost Alchemy' book.*

Chapter Six – Take a Deep Breath

Following the last chapter, I thought I'd give you a 'peek behind the curtain' to demonstrate the importance of getting a correct diagnosis. To do this, I'm going to talk you through a rather challenging time of my life, when getting an accurate diagnosis for a health problem made a huge difference to my quality of life.

A number of years ago, I noticed that I was struggling to breathe normally. It wasn't an obvious emergency (the "go directly to A&E" type of thing) because it developed gradually over time.

My breathing was becoming more laboured, and I was frequently short of breath when I was active.

This was a real problem in normal everyday life, but also for my job, because I was working at the time as a professional magician (yes, really).

During my shows, I found that I was struggling to keep my high energy levels up. To successfully engage and entertain people during a magic show takes a heck of a lot of focused energy. To the audience, it should look effortless. Behind the scenes, there is a *lot* of work going on!

Due to my shortness of breath, I had to slow down the pace of my show, the pace I spoke at and the amount I moved around on stage.

Not only did it affect the way I did my shows, it also meant that I was far more tired after each show than I should have been. Each show was taking far more out of me than previously.

I was performing an average of 4-6 shows every weekend, so it didn't take long before I was *really* struggling with breathing and energy.

Beyond exhausted

Over a period of months, my shortness of breath became so bad that I could no longer walk 20 metres down our road without being absolutely wiped out, beyond exhausted.

In short, it was a horrible time.

To top it off, this happened quite near the time our son was diagnosed with leukaemia. While he was in hospital having important, life-saving treatment, and we had all the pressures, exhaustion and emotional strain from that, I was struggling to breathe.

At night, I would lie down and wonder if I was going to make it through to the morning because I just could not breathe.

I started having to sleep with an extra pillow at night. Then two extra pillows. Before long I was sitting almost upright in bed at night, because it was the only position I could breathe in.

As you can hopefully imagine, this really wasn't a particularly pleasant thing to go through!

I had seen my local doctor a number of times, and they tried a few different things, but nothing helped. Their diagnosis started as a chest infection, then moved to “possibly asthma” over a few months.

However, regardless of the antibiotics or inhalers they prescribed me, my symptoms remained. I still struggled to breathe.

Inhaler time!

To cut a long story short, I was given different inhalers to try over a period of months to hopefully resolve the symptoms I had, as the doctor thought I may have asthma (despite having no history of asthma).

Different asthma inhalers are different colours, and I tried them all. Blue (*salbutamol*) did nothing to relieve my symptoms. Nor did brown (*beclomethasone*) or purple (*seretide*).

In fact, I was just struggling more as time went on.

It was *so* frustrating because it was impacting every aspect of life; family, work, ability to exercise – *everything.*

Long-term sleep deprivation and the ongoing mental and emotional pressures of supporting our son through his chemotherapy was not a good combination.

I was absolutely ragged, running on empty.

For a long time.

A different approach

After 12 months of this, I saw a different doctor. They took a different approach, knowing that they needed to get a firm diagnosis to be able to provide me with the treatment I needed.

Rather than continuing to try treatments that clearly weren't working, they started talking to the respiratory specialists in the local hospital. They asked for their advice about what diagnostic tests and investigations would be helpful.

They then referred me to the hospital for expert investigation by the respiratory specialists.

By the time I had my appointment with the respiratory consultant, they had enough information there to say that it looked like I had asthma but that a few further specialist tests would be needed to confirm this diagnosis.

These tests were arranged and carried out within a matter of weeks, and a diagnosis of adult-onset asthma was confirmed.

With this diagnosis, the respiratory consultant was able to prescribe me two new inhalers.

Far different to the ones I'd tried previously, these were new and worked a slightly different way.

And (most importantly) they worked!

When I started using these new inhalers, things turned around dramatically. I went from having no energy and struggling to breathe to being able to exercise again and to lie down in bed with only one pillow.

Within four months of getting the correct treatment, I completed my first 100km ultramarathon to raise money for CLIC Sargent.

I had the energy to engage with family and I was able to be there for my son in the hospital. I had the energy I needed to perform my magic shows normally again.

I got my life back.

During all the months I'd been struggling with my breathing, it had been tough, and I had become quite depressed about it. After all, I thought to myself, what good was I when I couldn't breathe?

But all it needed was an accurate diagnosis so that the right treatment could be arranged.

The same is true for business.

Things *can* change

Sometimes things can be tough. They can be challenging. You might think that you've tried everything to 'fix' a problem, but the pesky problem is still there, draining your energy.

It can be *annoying*.

It can be *frustrating*.

It can be *depressing*.

But maybe you just need an accurate diagnosis of the problem. Perhaps you need to take a different approach to working out what is causing the problem.

When I got the right treatment for my asthma, my breathing was changed almost overnight from uncontrolled to controlled; unmanaged to managed.

From struggle to easy.

Could the right diagnosis have the same effect on your business challenges?

Chapter Seven – Treatment

Continuing our healthcare-based approach to business and marketing, let's assume that you now have an accurate diagnosis. You know *exactly* what is causing your symptoms, your business problems.

As has been said repeatedly in this book up to this point, it is *only* when you have an accurate diagnosis that you can tailor the correct treatment for your business marketing.

At this point, I'd like to sound a word of caution which I first heard a number of years ago, then again more recently from Tom Beal (a.k.a. "*The Simplifier*"). Whether talking about treatments for business or marketing problems, there is no place for personal bias or personal arrogance. In other words:

Would you rather be right or rich?

As Joel Bauer says, "**Your ego is not your amigo**!"

If you have an accurate diagnosis, it is important that you treat the problem that has been diagnosed, not the one you want it to have been. The treatment you use must be the best one for *that* problem (which may not always be the one you *want* to use due to personal preference/price/difficulty of implementation etc.).

Treatment needs to be based on the data, not personal preference

While it can be easy to agree with this idea in theory, I know how hard it can sometimes be to implement it in real life! We all have our personal preferences, both in life and in business.

Just as one person may prefer coffee over tea, or cereal over fruit for breakfast, one marketer may favour email marketing over SEO while another may have a bias towards mailing marketing postcards versus making outbound phone calls.

Neither is in and of itself wrong or right. It all depends on the *symptoms*, the *diagnosis* and the *treatment plan that will deliver the best results.*

You've probably heard this said previously:

**When you're a hammer,
every problem is a nail**

Be sure *you* don't approach every business problem with a 'hammer-meet-nail' mentality!

Whether you are a marketer or business owner, copywriter or ad person, your personal preference *must* come lower down in the priority scale than **doing what is best for the business**.

One of the challenges this brings up is that many of us don't want to admit that we don't know the answer to something. It's all too easy to try to bluff our way through.

But isn't the wise, healthy thing to admit what we *don't* know? To admit there are even things that we don't yet know that we don't know?! To seek help and advice from people who *do* know?

This is one of the reasons why in healthcare very often you have an MDT - a multidisciplinary team. This is a group of experts in different disciplines who meet to discuss treatment options for certain patients.

For example, in an MDT you may have a:

- Pain relief consultant
- Oncology consultant
- Psychologist
- Nurse Specialist
- Dietician

- Physiotherapist

This 'whole team' approach helps to ensure that any treatment is carefully monitored, assessed and adjusted if needed.

Throughout our son's chemotherapy treatment, it was incredibly reassuring to know that he had a team of specialists looking out for him, to make sure he always received the best possible treatment and care (even through all the different side effects and problems he experienced – and there were *many*).

Gut instinct

At one stage during our son's treatment, he developed a very serious condition called *Typhlitis*, inflammation of the caecum (the beginning of the large intestine). His body needed to have complete gut rest, which meant that he had to have his nutrition through IV supply.

When this was first diagnosed, I remember the oncology consultant said that they would need to discuss the best way forward within the MDT.

Up to that point in his treatment, all the different problems and side effects that chemotherapy had created had been managed within well-rehearsed and well-known protocols that the oncology team were experienced in using.

This was the first problem we'd known the oncology team to be a bit surprised by. And so, they talked with the gastrointestinal consultants and the dieticians to ensure our son received treatment that was safe for him and that would help him to recover.

We experienced first-hand the value of a multidisciplinary team in healthcare.

Do *you* have a team of experts like this in your business? (Or, if you're a one-man business, do you have an external team you can call upon if needed?)

A note of caution: If you do have a 'Marketing MDT', be sure that it doesn't become 'just another meeting', where ideas are batted around *ad infinitum* with no firm action being taken directly afterwards.

If you're going to go to the effort (and often expense) of talking with specialists in other fields, whether copywriting or SEO, web design or user experience (UX), the end results should be having an effective treatment plan where the first steps can be taken immediately.

As Joe Vitale says:

"Money loves speed"

The world is full of businesses that treat marketing (and the business itself) as something that can be done at a leisurely pace. No deadlines, no urgency and no accountability for implementing ideas.

A healthy company is one where speed of implementation is a fundamental assumption.

If you're involved in a serious road traffic accident (RTA) and are bleeding profusely from your leg as a result, you want the paramedics who attend the scene to act as soon as they have assessed the situation and have determined the problem – not an hour later, after they've had a coffee while discussing how they plan to stop your bleeding with their colleagues!

An overly exaggerated picture? Of course – you know that's how I work (and it's also much more likely that you'll remember a ridiculous or exaggerated situation).

Treatment options

In medical terms, treatments are often split into two different types; operative and non-operative.

Non-operative includes treatments like physiotherapy, pain relief medication or an injection of a corticosteroid. Many conditions are usually treated first with non-operative treatments.

Operative treatments are more invasive, involving some type of surgery. Even this can be further sub-divided though, as there are many different approaches to surgery.

Traditional 'open' surgery will usually require a larger cut (incision) made in the skin, to gain access to the relevant part of the body.

Keyhole surgery involves making a few small cuts in the skin, then inserting specialist surgical tools through these gaps to carry out the surgery. This approach will often mean reduced pain, less visible scarring and a faster recovery.

At the time of writing, Robotic-Arm Assisted Surgery is becoming more common in certain types of operation.

The focus of any treatment is...

Whichever treatment is used, the underlying focus is always the same - to help somebody get better. If the patient is still unwell after treatment, it would be silly to suggest that their treatment had been successful.

Throughout our son's 3.5 years of treatment, his treatment was regularly monitored (at hourly, daily, weekly and monthly intervals, depending on his health at the time) and adjusted as needed.

The same is true in business. If treatment for a business problem does not work, it is of no use to that business. The approach to treatment will need to be adjusted, monitored and adjusted again. Sometimes a completely different treatment may be needed.

Yet every day, tens of thousands of businesses around the world are being advised to use the wrong treatment for their problem.

The failure rate of business treatments would be unacceptable in a hospital setting (indeed the surgeons would probably end up being struck off the medical register if their success rate was as low as that of many business consultants and consultancy firms!)

The whole point of healthy marketing is to get you in front of the right person, who will benefit from what you are offering *and* who can afford to pay what you charge.

To be able to **sell the right thing to the right person at the right time**.

While ‘hard selling’ has a bad reputation, this is because it has often been done in the wrong way. Pressuring somebody to buy something that they do not need and that will be of no value to them is wrong, plain and simple. It is as unconscionable as a doctor pressuring a patient to have a hip replacement when their natural hips are perfectly healthy and functioning properly.

Having said that, I *am* a big believer in hard selling IF (and only if) what you have is truly of value to that person, and if it would be the right choice for them and where their business is today.

If you have something that is truly valuable to a business, that will add far more value to them than what you are charging, and if it is better than anything else out there, it is your moral obligation to sell ‘hard’ to them.

A successful sale means they will get the *best* solution for their needs, at a good price, while avoiding buying an inferior solution from a competitor that won’t provide them with anywhere near the value your solution will deliver to them.

Avoid ‘Fake Treatment’ Scams

Unfortunately, you don't have to look far to find business owners or marketers with horror stories of being mis-sold poor, ineffective, incorrect treatments.

The proliferation of online advertising has helped to ratchet this up a notch (or five!). So much confusion exists around online advertising - much of it by design, due to the big companies who offer these services making it difficult to know what is *really* working.

While the scope, scale and type of these scams is ever-changing, the primary way of detecting and avoiding them remains the same – **do your due diligence**.

If you receive an email in your Inbox from an unknown sender (often using a free email address!) offering to get you onto page one of Google®, your alarm bells should be ringing loudly enough that you mark the email as spam and quickly delete it.

Just as there are *healthy* ways of improving your position in search engine listings, there are unhealthy ways. Generally, the unhealthy ways are sold as a quick and easy fix while the healthy approaches often have a longer-term focus.

While 'quick and easy' sounds extremely enticing (and explains why so many otherwise intelligent people continue to fall for it), if you try to shortcut a healthy marketing process, you will often pay the price further down the road.

You *don't* want to be a business owner or marketer who spends money, time, effort and energy on so-called 'marketing treatments' that turn out to be merely a placebo.

The Time-Tested Principle of Principles

Whichever treatment you use to improve the health of your business and your marketing, you want to make sure that it is reliable. For this reason, I always advise people to focus on *principles*.

Principles have been tried and tested over time. They are not tactics that have been made up on the spot, or the latest 'must have' marketing gimmick that EVERYONE(!) is using.

As has already been mentioned in this chapter, one of the key principles to focus on is that of delivering value to your clients (what a concept!).

Other principles include:

- Having more money coming IN to your business than you have going OUT
- Focusing on results
- Focusing on business inputs rather than business outputs (i.e. things you can control vs. things you cannot control)

- Clarity
- Frameworks vs. systems

Common Business Treatments

The exact treatment you apply to your business marketing will depend upon the diagnosis.

Listed below are some common treatment options for your consideration.

- Testing a different headline
- Testing a different offer
- Making a price change (lowering or raising)
- Plugging 'leaky holes' in your business systems
- Adding a bonus to a product
- Adding or changing an upsell
- Changing (or introducing for the first time) a backend offer
- Introducing a follow-up system (one for leads, one for buyers)
- Developing a reliable, repeatable sales process
- Full website redevelopment
- Creation (or re-design) of a comprehensive lead generation system
- Developing a testimonial and/or referral system
- Introducing an email marketing campaign

- Employing more staff to ensure a faster response to enquiries
- Replacing unproductive staff with productive new hires
- Changing from a sales-focused business to a marketing-focused business
- Introducing a new service or product to the market
- Removing a service or product from the market
- Replacing a service or product with a new and superior one
- Offering a payment plan (or removing/replacing a current one)
- Advertising in a different media or business category
- Changing your marketing to attract a different type of client
- Testing bundling services or products together

A Final Warning About Treatments

I would be remiss if I failed to mention the potential danger of using a 'one-stop' approach to marketing.

There are many individuals and companies who offer "every marketing solution in the world, all under one roof"!

I would strongly caution against using ONE person or ONE company for all your business marketing.

(I say this as somebody who provides marketing services to companies, so I'm writing myself out of potential business – that's because I genuinely believe it is the correct, *healthy* approach.)

If you required knee surgery, you would probably want to have the surgery carried out by a knee specialist.

You would *not* want a neurosurgeon to carry it out. While a neurosurgeon is certainly an expert in their field, neurosurgery is very different to knee surgery!

If for some reason you did see a neurosurgeon for a knee problem, they would refer you to a knee specialist colleague, knowing that they would be the best person to help you.

<u>They know where the boundaries are for their area of expertise.</u>

Choosing to work with a marketing agency can often feel like walking into a group of doctors and asking if any of them can help you with an ankle problem, them looking at one another, and then the least busy one being volunteered to help you.

Jack of All Trades, Master of None

There are many (*many*!) things that I am NOT an expert in.

For example, I am not (nor do I pretend to be) an expert in search engine optimisation (SEO). I could probably do a pretty good job of blagging my way into working as an SEO specialist, but I would be doing a disservice to the people hiring me.

For me, it would be unethical to promote myself as an expert in an area where I am most definitely *not* an expert.

Yet there are many individuals and companies advertising themselves as SEO experts, and charging (often exorbitant) fees for their services.

Some may be '*okay*'.

Some may be *brilliant*.

Many will be *awful*.

It's a similar situation within my area of expertise: using words to communicate more persuasively. There are many people promoting themselves as copywriters whose only qualification is that they have a degree in English Language.

They can write nicely, with perfect grammar.

But can they sell a product or service using their words?

Do they know how to structure a sales letter?

Have they studied the past masters of direct-response copywriting, who relied on and used principles to get sales?

For many of them, the answer to those questions would be a big “NO”.

Often, copywriting in a bigger agency will be farmed out to the newest hire, who may have little or no experience in commercial writing *and* who is juggling twenty other jobs, all with equally pressing deadlines.

Is that really the way you want to have the content you’re paying for created?

I hope not.

Many years ago, I heard Dan Kennedy talk about salespeople who “sold only in their memories and in other people’s nightmares!”

Replace ‘salespeople’ with ‘marketer, ‘copywriter’, ‘SEO specialist’ etc., and you can see what you most definitely want to avoid.

When considering any marketing treatment, always make sure that you have the best person for that specific treatment working on it.

An expert is always paid more than a generalist for a reason – because they are an *expert*.

Chapter Eight – I Was NOT Expecting That!

The movies and TV lied to me.

The very first time I went into an operating theatre while working as a diagnostic radiographer in the NHS, I was *shocked.*

In every TV show or film I had watched, whenever a scene involved a character needing surgery, the operating theatre was always shown as being a very serious, quiet place.

The only person who ever spoke was the surgeon who was carrying out the operation.

The only noises heard were the quiet beeping, humming and whirring of the anaesthetist's equipment as it kept the patient breathing artificially.

You can imagine my surprise when I discovered that an operating theatre was actually a *very* different environment to the one I had seen on screen.

As I trundled the C-arm of the portable imaging equipment into the theatre, I was greeted by the noise of a radio playing and the relaxed chatter of the theatre staff as they made sure everything was prepared, in place and ready before the patient arrived from the ward.

While I plugged in the cable connecting the C-arm and the monitor to one another, I chatted with the staff about what they'd been up to at the weekend, and about how their kids were getting on at school.

Of course, once the surgery began, the atmosphere was always professional. The surgeon was focused on their work, the theatre nurse was focused on the surgeon, the anaesthetist was focused on the patient, and I was focused on getting the best imaging possible whenever it was needed by the surgeon.

But even though the way the surgeon and nurse scrubbed up before the surgery, and the way they were helped into their surgical gowns by other staff, was like the process shown on TV, the actual working environment during the surgery was very different to what many would assume it to be.

If you had been allowed to walk past the operating theatre and peek through the small circular window, you would have seen what you would have expected to see. From a distance and at a quick glance, it would have looked remarkably like the scenes shown on TV.

But what you would have seen was an incomplete picture.

During the years I worked as a radiographer, I spent a lot of time in operating theatres, wearing surgical scrubs, a surgical cap and surgical mask.

I saw surgeon's egos get the better of them, as they exploded at nursing staff who weren't as quick at delivering the right surgical tools as the surgeon wanted them to be.

(As an aside, I always found orthopaedic surgeons to be the most likely to get frustrated or angry, while the urological surgeons were always the most relaxed and down-to-earth!)

I saw the strain in the eyes of the surgeon as they battled to fix shattered bones together as precisely as possible.

I shared the exhaustion of the theatre staff as we all stood in the operating theatre at 3am following an emergency operation for a patient who had been involved in a road traffic accident late at night.

I remember muttering with the other theatre staff at 1pm on Christmas Day, when we'd all been called in for an emergency operation that turned out to be anything but 'urgent'.

The experience I gained during that time makes me smile every time I now see a 'surgery scene' in a TV episode or in a movie. While there is sometimes a bit of similarity to the real thing, there is an awful lot that is nowhere near the reality.

A Peek Below the Surface

It can be the same in business.

Whatever industry you are in, you may have gone into it with certain expectations of how things were done, how decisions were made, and how profit was generated.

While your assumptions and expectations may have been correct, it is more likely that they only reflected a small percentage of what *really* goes on in your business.

Similarly, if you look at a 'successful' businessperson (this is usually one who is idolised by the media and younger marketers on social media), your perception may be very different if it is only a surface level look vs. a deep dive below the surface.

When you take a deep dive into any business or industry, or you look below the surface of any hugely successful businessperson, you will often see something very different to what is visible on the surface.

Very often, you will discover that the things you thought were the priorities, the essential things, aren't really that important or essential.

What you *thought* was the secret of their success may turn out to be anything but.

When I was training as a diagnostic radiographer, a large part of the degree was focused on learning about the physics of X-rays and how radiography equipment worked. A lot of time was also spent on learning about human anatomy and physiology.

For my job, it was of course important to know what the different bones in the body were. That information was *necessary* for the job.

But physics?

- Did I really need that knowledge on a day-to-day basis, while actually doing the job?

- When I walked into the A&E 'crash room' to take X-rays of an unconscious, badly injured patient, did the rest of the medical team call me in because of my knowledge about physics?

- Did they rely on me because I could explain how the X-ray film was going to be developed, from X-ray cassette (I'm old – it's all produced digitally now!) to final image on the film?

No.

The most important part of the job was that I could provide them with the best possible image so that an accurate diagnosis could be made.

That was the priority.

Of course, there are certain legal requirements for qualifying and being able to work as a diagnostic radiographer in the UK. Similar legal requirements exist for many other jobs, such as solicitors, police officers, pharmacists, nurses, physiotherapists and occupational therapists.

There are certain things you are obligated to learn about and to know. Many jobs have ongoing personal development as a requirement of their work.

This is all of course as it should be.

BUT…(and this is my big "*butt*"!)…many of the things you learn as part of your job aren't needed each and every day. They are not an essential part of your daily work.

To be slightly controversial (*I've managed to make it this far without being controversial!),* a lot of marketing theory that is taught nowadays and taken as absolute truth is not necessarily correct.

While it may read well on paper, and might even allow you to tick a box on a random form to show compliance of learning objectives, when used in the real world it will often fail – and fail *miserably.*

As has been said, <u>no battle plan survives first contact with the enemy</u>!

Despite the above tirade, please know that I am not anti-theory. Instead, I am anti-useless!

Frameworks over Systems

I am a big proponent of frameworks over systems:

A *system* tends to be more rigid, fixed, inflexible. 'Yes' or 'No'. 'Left' or 'right'. There is often very little nuance.

A *framework* is malleable, flexible, liberating, yet still able to provide structure and strength.

How does this apply to marketing?

As a marketer, there are certain things it is helpful to know. Things like:

- What makes a good headline?
- The words that help to persuade and influence
- How to design a print ad to heighten its effectiveness
- How to structure a sales letter or website sales page to increase its effectiveness

I would argue that it is far more valuable to have:

- An understanding of **human psychology** *(particularly the psychology of change)*
- A deep understanding of <u>buying patterns and behaviours</u>
- Successful experience of **direct (i.e. face-to-face) selling**
- An understanding of your industry, your business and your customers

These are things that cannot be learned just from books. They can't be understood and implemented only by theoretical analysis or logic.

These things can all be useful, and there is a time and a place for them. <u>I am not telling you to throw logic or analysis out of the window.</u>

I AM telling you that to be a healthy marketer you need to roll your sleeves up, put your boots on the ground, walk into the operating theatre and get some 'down and dirty' experience in the real world.

There is *no* shortcut to real-world experience.

In so many aspects of life, especially for marketing, you can read all the books you want.

(*I am fully aware of the irony of including that last sentence in a marketing book!*)

I am not saying don't read books. Books are a HUGE part of my life. I believe firmly in what Zig Ziglar said many years ago:

**"Poor people have large TVs.
Rich people have large libraries."**

I live my life by that quote.

I have many books in my house. My wife and I both love reading.

You can learn a lot from books.

But the power of reading a business book is in applying and implementing the theory you have learned in your actual job.

This is how you discover what really works.

This is where the 'marketing magic' happens.

At the very beginning of this chapter, I explained how different operating theatres are in hospitals compared to how they are portrayed in TV shows and movies.

And so it is with marketing.

Sometimes, your marketing reality will be *very* different to what you may have imagined after reading a marketing or copywriting book.

It will often be very different to what you see your competitors doing.

When you experience this alternate reality, you need to adjust your expectations, change your approach and then just get on with it.

You need to walk into the metaphorical operating theatre of your business and **get the job done**.

Chapter Nine – Recovery

Any doctor, nurse, physiotherapist - *anyone* involved in healthcare or fitness - will tell you that allowing sufficient time for recovery is crucial to peak performance.

If you try to rush your recovery from an injury, you will often cause yourself more damage, possibly permanent. At the very least, you will slow down the speed of your recovery.

Similarly, if you continually exercise without giving yourself adequate time to rest and recover, you increase the risk of injuring yourself and run the risk of further reducing your performance. (*A personal story of this can be read in the next chapter.)*

Even a healthy person needs a certain amount of sleep each day to give their body time to rest and recover, to ensure peak performance is achievable the next day. This is a fundamental principle of health; one you skip at your own peril.

Hurry Up and Slow Down!

Now, this is all well and good in theory – as words printed in a book – but what does this mean in reality?

Let's look at healthcare first, business second.

Following any type of medical treatment, you will need to give yourself adequate space and time to heal and recover properly. While you may see some improvement immediately after treatment, it often takes time to experience the full benefits.

For example, somebody who has had total hip replacement surgery may be mobilising safely after a week or two, but it could take a further 6 – 12 months for them to see the full benefits of their surgery…

<u>…if they follow the rehabilitation exercises and guidance they have been given.</u>

If they try to rush their recovery, literally running before they can walk, they may experience complications and possibly never get the full benefits of the surgery they would have hoped for.

A proper recovery ensures all the necessary muscles, ligaments and tendons are safely strengthened. Range of motion, flexibility and function in the joint can be slowly and safely tested and improved over time.

An 'instant fix' is not possible for such a major operation. While the operation itself to replace the damaged joint with an artificial one may only be a few hours, the recovery will take longer.

'Fast' Isn't *Always* 'Best'

The quote above may at first seem to go against my comment in an earlier chapter that "*money loves speed*", but both these quotes complement one another. It's all about context.

Money loves speed…when speed involves the *right* things being done, in the *right* way and at the *ideal pace*. After all, the quickest way to get rich is to rob a bank. Hopefully you'd agree that it's also not the wisest way to get or to stay rich!

As you can probably guess, this holds true for business.

If your business has been *un*healthy for a long time, it will take time to recover fully, even after you have treated the underlying cause(s). The speed – and degree - of the recovery will depend on several variables, including the severity of the underlying problem and the effectiveness of the treatment used.

If your business has been unhealthy for a long time, the treatment needed will probably be quite extensive. As the treatment starts having an effect, you will begin to see improvements in the health of your business.

These improvements will not usually be instant (although they *may* be in some cases). Often, it will take time for those improvements to really have a noticeable effect – for the treatment to deliver the optimal results.

As I write this, I am extremely aware that I am one of the last people to tell you to be patient and to wait for results – I want to see results NOW.

In fact, I want to see them YESTERDAY!

However, life has shown me – and continues to show me – that proper, healthy success cannot be rushed or artificially sped up. <u>Sometimes, you've just got to let the process run.</u>

Although it seems a bit unusual to include this in a book about healthy marketing, a quote from the military about weapon handling seems appropriate at this point:

"Slow is smooth, smooth is fast."

Or as my grandparents used to tell me, "Haste makes waste."

As part of a marketing project I was hired for by a smart company [THIS IS A SUBTLE HINT THAT YOU TOO, DEAR READER, SHOULD HIRE ME], I talked with a lot of orthopaedic consultants who specialised in hip surgery.

I was amazed when they told me that patients who have had total hip replacement surgery will often be mobilising the same day as their operation, often within a few hours of their surgery.

Once they have recovered fully from the anaesthetic, the physiotherapy team will visit with them and help them to start moving, because the data shows that the sooner they start mobilising after surgery, the better it often is for their long-term recovery.

My kids like to remind me that I am *very old* (at the time of writing this, I am 43!), but when I worked as a radiographer people were most definitely <u>not</u> expected to mobilise the same day as their hip surgery. Back then, it was measured in days, not *hours*.

One thing to remember is that the recovery process starts immediately after treatment. The full results and benefits of the treatment may take time, but the recovery process begins straight away.

If you have a medical problem requiring prescription medicine, the doctor will not normally tell you to start taking the medication in six months' time – you will usually be told to start taking it the same day that it is prescribed.

Just as you need to listen to your body as you recover from a physical illness, so you need to 'listen' to your business as it recovers from a problem. 'Listening' in this case involves looking carefully at certain metrics, the key numbers in your business, each day - without fail.

You need to have an acute awareness of *what* is going on in your business at every stage of the recovery. This way, if any adjustments or changes are needed at any point to aid or improve the extent or speed of recovery, you will be able to make them quickly.

Failure is an Event, not a Death Sentence

At this point, I'd like to press the 'pause' button on the business marketing aspect of this book and transition to a bit more of a personal reflection. If this next 'bit' is irrelevant to you, that's great – please jump to the next chapter. If it *is* relevant to you, I hope that when you read the following it is at exactly the right time for you to hear what I have to tell you.

If your business is in recovery mode, it is important that you remember that 'failure' of any kind – whether in business or in your personal life - is only an event.

- It is not *final*
- It is not *irreversible*
- It is not a *judgement on you as a person*

You tried something. It didn't work. You can try again.

If you look carefully at any person who is generally perceived as 'successful' – whether in business, sports, politics etc. - you will very often discover that they have had failures in the past; often very big failures.

Those failures have not stopped them moving forward.

The same holds true for business.

- Just because you didn't close a sale in your last meeting does not mean you won't close in your next meeting
- A failed product launch does not mean that your next product launch will not succeed

- Missing your business goals for one month does not mean you won't meet them next month

And so it goes…

Failure is an event.

That is all.

You can pick yourself up, learn from it and continue moving forward.

The very best thing you can do after a failure is to *immediately* get straight back up and to keep going.

As I used to be told, "You fall off a horse, the first thing you do is to get straight back on the horse." (Admittedly this was a bit odd, as I've never owned a horse and to this day have never ridden a horse. Go figure!)

The main takeaway of this chapter is to be kind to yourself and to give yourself and your business the time needed to recover from all that has gone before.

Tomorrow is another day. Tomorrow can be a better day.

Tomorrow *will* be a better day.

Chapter Ten – Ultramarathons

The first year of our son's chemotherapy treatment, I decided to raise money for CLIC Sargent, a charity in the UK that supports children and families affected by childhood cancer. They were a big support to us throughout his treatment, and I wanted to do something – *anything* – to show my appreciation of the work they did.

I Laugh at 5km and 10km Events

I had seen the growing popularity of 5km and 10km charity events, and being the ~~idiot~~ kind of person I am, decided I wanted to do something different to the majority (*incidentally, this is an excellent approach to take with marketing*).

A few online searches later, I discovered something that excited and terrified me in equal measure – a 100km ultramarathon. I knew immediately that this was exactly the type of fundraising event I was looking for.

100km.

That's a bit harder to ignore than the 'standard' 5km and 10km events, isn't it?

Yep, that was big enough to stop people in their tracks.

The company running this event, Action Challenge, offered a number of ultramarathons throughout the year, and in different locations. I decided to sign up for their **London to Brighton 100km Ultramarathon**, as it meant my wider family, most of whom lived in Surrey, would all be able to come and cheer me on.

Now I am somebody who finds it hard to motivate myself unless I have a definite goal. As soon as I signed up to walk the 100km to raise money for CLIC Sargent, my brain switched instantly into 'training mode'.

When I signed up to the ultramarathon, I knew that I wasn't going to run it – instead, I would aim to walk it all in one go, without stopping overnight. To me, that would be a real achievement – particularly with all we were going through as a family at the time.

My therapy

My training walks became my therapy, a way for me to switch off temporarily from the pressures, emotions, stresses and sadness that often threatened to engulf me during our son's treatment. Those training walks became windows of opportunity and helped me to feel that I was finally doing something practical to say "Thank You" to CLIC Sargent and the staff we saw each day at the hospital.

Once I'd signed up to the 100km, I was deeply touched when one of my brothers, my brother-in-law and a friend all also signed up to walk it with me, as a way of showing solidarity in such a testing time.

My training walks progressed from one hour to two hours. Then three to four hours. Before long, I was walking for much longer periods, without too many aches and pains (they came later!). I would walk from our house to the children's hospital, spend the day with our son, then walk back home again.

I timed my walks to fit around our daughter's school day, our son's different hospital admissions and treatments and my work commitments. Somehow, we managed to make it work (although looking back on it now, I am not sure how!).

As my body adapted and adjusted to the increased training I was doing, my walks became longer. The longest training walk I did before the event itself was around 40km – constrained by available time from doing anything longer than that. The skin on my feet toughened up, so I was hoping to avoid blisters during the event.

One Down. Let's Do Two More!

The actual event itself seemed to come around much sooner than anticipated. And sure enough, the training paid off – joined by my brother, brother-in-law and friend, we walked 100km non-stop, starting in the morning, walking all day and through the night, finishing around 7am the next morning.

We were all tired, both emotionally and physically, but we had done it - and had raised a good amount of money for charity in the process!

Fast forward a few weeks, and I had apparently been bitten by the ultramarathon bug. I decided I'd like to do the London to Brighton 100km again the following year – and my wife wanted to do it with me!

So, we both signed up for the following year's event. I decided I wanted to try to complete TWO ultramarathons, so also signed up to the Cotswold Way 100km Challenge, which was being held about 6 weeks after the London to Brighton 100km. I figured that six weeks between the events would be plenty of time for me to recover.

Boy, was I wrong!

Over the next few months, my wife and I somehow managed to juggle work, family life, our son's ongoing chemotherapy and training walks with one another. (Again, looking back on it now, I really have no idea how we managed to do this. I'll say it was largely due to my wife's awesomeness!)

The Second Ultramarathon

Before we knew it, my wife and I were on the starting line for the London to Brighton 100km. Fast forward 20 hours, and we arrived in Brighton the next morning, hand in hand – weary but content.

It was lovely walking with my wife on the second ultramarathon. We had been, and still were, going through such a lot together as a family with the ups and downs of our son's treatment. Being able to walk with one another, encouraging and supporting each other as needed, was truly special.

Unfortunately, my wife did end up with blisters that were so nasty she needed several trips to the podiatrist. Her feet eventually recovered – but it did take a while!

Recovery – I Missed You

After that London to Brighton 100km, I had six weeks before I would be walking the next ultramarathon, the Cotswold Way Challenge.

I was tired and needed a lot of time to recover and re-energise, both physically and mentally. I didn't really appreciate just how long it takes to fully recover from walking 100km. A mark of how tired I was is that I didn't manage any training walks until the week leading up to the Cotswold Way Challenge. Maybe not the best preparation!

And so, six weeks later, I was standing in the historic city of Bath and about to cross the starting line for the Cotswold Way Challenge.

Almost as soon as I started the event, I knew that I was in trouble. I felt still so physically tired that every step from the 2km mark onwards was exhausting. I felt like I was walking through treacle with weights on my boots.

Oh dear.

Due to my tiredness, I hadn't looked very carefully at the terrain for this walk. After all, I figured that one 100km would be just like another.

It turns out that I was wrong about this.

While the London to Brighton 100km is fairly flat, with only one big hill (Ditchling Beacon) towards the end, the Cotswold Way Challenge was much hillier. In fact, it was very, *very* hilly.

I hadn't focused on hill walking during any of my previous training, and my legs still weren't fully recovered from the previous ultramarathon.

Long story short, there was no way my body was capable of getting me around 100km of hilly countryside. I struggled through 50km, but then decided to withdraw from the event.

Even though I was disappointed, I knew that I was likely to cause serious injury if I continued to force myself around the route. It was a tough call to make, but it was absolutely the right choice.

What Had Gone Wrong?

In the last chapter, we looked at the importance of recovery. That chapter was written with my own harsh experience in the Cotswold Way Challenge firmly in my mind!

Recovery – proper, full recovery – is crucial to performance.

I had not given myself anywhere near enough time to recover from one 100km before trying to do another one. My body let me know pretty quickly though!

I also hadn't been properly prepared for the amount of hill walking required. With most of my training being done on fairly flat terrain, I just didn't have enough power in my legs to get up and down so many hills.

I Shall Come Back Stronger!

Disappointed with having to drop out of the Cotswold Way Challenge, I plotted my ultramarathon return for the following year.

I deliberately chose the one that was regarded as the toughest one Action Challenge ran – the Jurassic Coast 100km. Running along the South Coast of England between Bournemouth and Bridport, this route had the highest total elevation of all their challenges – in short, it was brutally hilly!

Now I like to try to learn from my mistakes. (Sometimes it takes me longer than I would like, but I will usually get there in the end!) I knew that to complete this challenge successfully, I would need to do a lot of hill walking during my training.

So for the next six months, I deliberately sought out the steepest hills I could get to and then walked up and down them as much as possible

I drove into Wales and walked up Pen Y Fan a number of times. I drove to Lynton and walked along the South West Coast Path, pushing myself up hills far steeper than I could find in Bristol.

Hill walking is both awful and exhilarating, horrible and great. At the start of my training, I was out of breath and struggling very quickly. As my body adapted and my legs became stronger, I was able to push myself harder as I walked up the hills.

I started lifting weights, focusing on squats and deadlifts to build up strength in my legs.

I did a *lot* of core exercises to strengthen my abdominal and back muscles.

I did countless pull-ups and press-ups to strengthen my upper body.

By the time the Jurassic Coast 100km Challenge came around, I was in the best shape of my life. Even though I knew it would be tough, I felt *ready*.

I had put the hard work in for months. Now it was time for the pay off.

The Price and The Prize

As I started the challenge, I knew pretty early on that my training had been a massive help. As I strode up each hill, walking poles and legs in perfect harmony, I told myself, "*This* was what all my training was for. *This* is the pay off."

For every prize we strive for, a price must be paid.

The price may be hours of weightlifting or hill walking, late nights studying old copywriting books or early mornings spent learning about SEO or sales techniques.

Whatever the prize is, the price must *always* be paid. In full.

As I walked the route, I noticed that most people taking part in the challenge would arrive at the foot of a hill and instantly slow down as they started uphill. Many of them stopped completely halfway up, sitting down to catch their breath and admire the view.

It was very easy to see the people who had put in the training and those who hadn't; to see those who had *paid the price* in advance.

I kept the same pace regardless of whether I was going uphill, downhill or was on the flat. My pace was consistent, each kilometre completed within 30 seconds of another.

I was well prepared, but I would be lying if I told you that it was easy.

It was still *hard work*, particularly from 80km onwards. A pebble beach towards the end (darn you Chesil Beach!) was HARD!

But I did it.

I had deliberately trained for months to be <u>comfortable with being uncomfortable.</u>

And it's the same in business. Nothing changes until you step out of your comfort zone.

If you're happy where you are and how your business is, it can be easy to relax and to stop pushing forward.

And that's fine.

But… there may be a competitor who *is* pushing hard, who *is* deliberately stepping outside of their comfort zone.

How long will you stay ahead of them?

If ‘hills’ appear in your business, will you be able to get up them? At what pace?

Are you preparing your business today for challenges *tomorrow*?

In business as in life, we constantly need to move forward. We need to push ourselves, to challenge ourselves to try new things.

We may fail.

Or we could succeed.

As I close this chapter, I’ll leave you with some questions to consider:

- What have you done today to improve your business?

- How about this week?

- This month?

- The last six months?

- The last year?

- What will you do tomorrow?

- Are any business goals you have set comfortable and fairly attainable, without *too* much effort? Or are they BIG goals where failure is possible?

Chapter Eleven –
Your Healthy Marketing Future

As we near the end of this book, I thought it would be helpful to take a step back from the words on the page and to look once more at the *big picture* of your business.

So far in this book we have:

- Explored the similarities between health, fitness and business
- Broken the standard healthcare pathway down into a simple process – Assessment, Diagnosis, Treatment and Recovery – and adapted these to help when thinking about the health of a business
- Been involved in an imaginary fall down the stairs!
- Joined me on a couple of 100km ultramarathons
- Discovered my sister's London Marathon hydration error(!)
- Walked the challenging, often painful, steps through my son's chemotherapy treatment

I said very clearly at the beginning of this book that it was *not* intended to be one of those marketing books that tries to force you into following **The 7 Essential Steps To Marketing Success and Untold Business Riches!**

This type of book tends to sell well, but often leaves the reader feeling either utterly dejected at their inability to measure up to the standards set out in the book *or* feeling completely confused about the real-life application of theoretical ideas.

Instead, this book has given you a framework, one that offers strength and structure while also giving flexibility and choice.

Healthy marketing is not a series of simplistic steps to work your way through until you arrive at '**Success Central**'. It is rather a way of *thinking differently* about business and marketing with a longer-term perspective.

Will This Clog or Cleanse Me?

Many years ago, my wife and I attended Tony Robbins' "Unleash The Power Within" seminar in London. While I found many parts of it helpful, one phrase in particular has stuck with me ever since.

Tony was talking about health, and he suggested that we should start asking ourselves a simple question every time we put something into our mouth – will this clog me or cleanse me?

Such a simple, easy-to-remember question, yet one that is also exceptionally profound.

Could you ask yourself the same question before rolling out a new marketing campaign or before developing a new product?

- Will this 'clog' or 'cleanse' my business?

- Will it help my business to grow, or could it cause damage and problems in the future?

- Is this the *healthiest option* for my business at this time?

The Value of Measuring

We have also looked at the importance of measuring certain numbers in your business. Whether that is on sales per day, cost per lead, cost per sale, number of referrals, refund rates etc., will be specific to each business.

The fact remains that if you want to improve anything, you need to measure it. How else can you know if there is any improvement?

By way of example, as somebody with asthma, I have an annual asthma review through my GP surgery. I also have a device to measure my peak flow, so I can keep track of it more regularly.

During our son's treatment, he was carefully monitored. Certain measurements like temperature, heart rate and oxygen saturation levels were recorded at various intervals. Blood samples were taken regularly to monitor the levels of platelets, neutrophils and white and red blood cells.

Now his treatment has finished, he still gets regular check-ups with the oncology team at the hospital.

These started as monthly reviews, then every two months, and now every six months. Soon they will move to 12-month reviews.

When he is an adult, he will be reviewed every five years.

Frequency

While you can improve anything that you measure or track, how often should you review things? Daily? Weekly? Monthly? Annually?

Let's turn our attention to an imaginary world-class 100m sprinter. How often do you think they would record their training times and compare them to previous times?

How closely do you think they monitor their food intake or their hydration? How about the quality of their sleep?

If they are a professional athlete, they will measure all these things very closely and very frequently indeed.

They can then examine the data to look for patterns, for changes, to see the difference that any changes have made. And – most importantly - they can make adjustments as needed.

<u>Remember, the more frequently you monitor something, the more likely you are to be able to improve it.</u>

If you review your business goals only once a year, it is unlikely you will meet them. Increasing the frequency of reviewing your goals increases the likelihood of meeting – or even exceeding - them.

Three important questions about measuring for you to mull over:

- *What* do you need to measure in your business?
- *Who* will be responsible for measuring it?
- *When* will they measure it?

Simple vs. Complex

Many of us look for the simplest way of doing something. While this isn't always wrong, it can often lead us down the wrong path.

For example, we may find ourselves asking:

- What is the ONE diet 'hack' that will help me to shed pounds?
- What is the ONE tablet I can take to treat my illness?
- What is the simplest way to get more followers on my social media accounts?
- How can I double my sales without doing more work?

I've used overly exaggerated examples above for clarity. There is something about human nature that causes us to default to 'Simple-Seeking Mode'!

Yet if we look closely, below the surface, of successful companies today, we will see complexity. Not only is complexity a central part of a successful business, it is often welcomed and deliberately sought after.

Building a healthy business involves *embracing* complexity.

By way of example, let's briefly look at Amazon.

Started originally as an online bookstore, it has been deliberately transformed over the years into a business with extremely complicated and numerous streams of income (remember the Diving Board and Parthenon comparison earlier in this book?).

With its complexity, Amazon has become exceptionally powerful, dominant and valuable. While smaller competitors try to eat away at its market share, they do so with simple tactics.

In a battle between simple and complex, complex will win every time.

Going Deep

To be a healthy marketer or owner of a healthy business means knowing your business and industry inside out.

You must keep your finger on the pulse of your industry, staying ahead of the curve, continually adapting for the future while also keeping things running smoothly in the present.

A good doctor will keep abreast of current and future trends in healthcare. They will read up about new medicines or surgical approaches. They will discuss future trends with their colleagues. They will be aware of healthcare legislation, both current and any currently progressing through the relevant authority.

As we close this book, a few questions for you to consider:

- How well do you know your business?
- How thoroughly do you know and understand your industry?
- How well do you know your customers and what motivates them?
- What changes is your industry facing?

- How are you planning to adapt your business in the next 1, 3, 5, 7, 10 years?

- What media is on the increase, and conversely, which is on the decrease?

- What challenges and opportunities will technology create in my business?

As you think about these questions, don't immediately go for the *simplest* answer. Instead, think deeply about them (after all, your competition is unlikely to spend much time thinking about them). Approach them as a student approaches an important exam – with care and focus.

Afterword - Flipping the Script

Throughout this book, I've used the idea of healthcare and a 'typical' medical treatment process to help think of your business and marketing as either *healthy* or *unhealthy*.

In these final few pages, I'd like to 'flip the script' and ask you to imagine that your business is now a hospital.

<u>That's right – you're going from 'patient' to 'healthcare provider' in just one page!</u>

Not only is your business now a hospital, but your clients are now patients, coming into your hospital because they need help with *something*.

With that picture firmly in your mind, I have a few questions for you to think about:

- What will their patient journey be like, from first arriving at your hospital through to their eventual discharge?

- Will you be able to provide them with the treatment they need without unnecessary delay?

- Or will they spend hours, days or even weeks being passed around from department to department, having countless investigations (many of them pointless)?

- Will the treatment(s) you give them work? Are they reliable?

- Are they likely to come back to you for help again if they develop another problem in the future?

- Will they be so impressed with the way you helped them that they will recommend your hospital to their friends and colleagues in the future?

With a Wave of the Magic Wand…

If we were to wave a magic wand (*I've managed to avoid alluding to my previous career as a professional magician for most of this book – this is the exception!*) and transform every business into a hospital in this way, many of them would have people standing outside promoting price-cuts for different treatments!

Some would have colourful banners advertising 30% off EVERY treatment.

Others would be promoting 'Two for One' offers (I'm thinking 'His and Hers' hip operations…).

Many would have doctors standing around in the reception area, asking anybody who ventures inside if they need help with anything.

A number would probably ask you to 'like' or 'follow' their social media pages (for no obvious reason or practical benefit to you).

A few of the larger hospitals might spend hundreds of thousands of pounds on a logo or brand 'refresh', in the certain knowledge that a new logo or brand revamp will get patients flocking in for assessment, diagnosis and treatment.

Others would send doctors out into the local neighbourhood, knocking on doors to see if people would like a new hip.

Some may be so surprised to have a patient walk in that they forget what they're supposed to do and will start offering treatments straight away. (You can imagine the conversation: "Good morning, madam. Would you like laser eye surgery today? How about a mole removal? Hip surgery? Please choose something – we're desperate!!")

Many other (possibly most?) businesses-turned-hospital would do *nothing*. Their doors would be opened, they would be fully staffed, and their diagnostic and surgical capabilities would be at the ready.

And they would just wait for somebody – *anybody* – to come into the hospital for help.

Reactive rather than proactive.

Hope rather than the assurance of a known, deliberate process to attract patients in.

Lazy.

How about you?

I *know* that your business is not in fact a hospital.

I appreciate that your clients are *not* patients.

But as a business, you are providing treatment of some kind, either by way of a service or a product.

How effective is the treatment you provide?

Would *you* choose to have treatment at your hospital if you needed it?

What could you do to make your hospital stand out from any others that offer similar treatments?

Does every patient coming to your hospital experience the same process?

Is the service your hospital provides fit for purpose?

Is it *healthy*?

Lightning Source UK Ltd.
Milton Keynes UK
UKHW011116280322
400719UK00001B/233